CW00502549

Spurgeon's Sermons on New Testament Women

Book One

C. H. Spurgeon Resources

A Classic Bible Study Library for Today
Commenting and Commentaries
Day by Day with C. H. Spurgeon (compiled by Al Bryant)
The Treasury of David (edited by David Otis Fuller)
Spurgeon's Sermon Illustrations
Spurgeon's Sermon Notes
Spurgeon's Sermons on the Cross of Christ
Spurgeon's Sermons on Old Testament Men • Book One
Spurgeon's Sermons on Old Testament Women • Book One
Spurgeon's Sermons on Prayer
Spurgeon's Sermons on the Resurrection of Christ
Spurgeon's Sermons on Soul-Winning

C. H. Spurgeon Sermon Series

Spurgeon's Sermons on New Testament Women

Book One

CHARLES HADDON SPURGEON

kregel
PUBLICATIONS

Grand Rapids, MI 49501

Spurgeon's Sermons on New Testament Women • Book One
by Charles H. Spurgeon.

Copyright © 1994 by Kregel Publications.

Published by Kregel Publications, a division of Kregel, Inc., P.O. Box 2607, Grand Rapids, MI 49501. Kregel Publications provides trusted, biblical publications for Christian growth and service. Your comments and suggestions are valued.

All rights reserved. No part of this book may be reproduced, stored in a retrieval system, or transmitted in any form or by any means—electronic, mechanical, photocopy, recording, or otherwise—without written permission of the publisher, except for brief quotations in printed reviews.

Cover artwork: Don Ellens
Cover and book design: Alan G. Hartman

Library of Congress Cataloging-in-Publication Data

Spurgeon, C. H. (Charles Haddon), 1834–1892.
[Sermons on New Testament women]
Spurgeon's Sermons on New Testament Women • Book One / by Charles H. Spurgeon.
p. cm.
1. Women in the Bible—Sermons. 2. Bible. N.T.—Sermons. 3. Sermons, English. I. Title. II. Series: Spurgeon, C. H. (Charles Haddon), 1834–1892. C. H. Spurgeon sermon series.
BS2445.S66 1994 220.9'2'082—dc20 94-17881
CIP

ISBN 0-8254-3782-2 (pbk.)

1 2 3 4 5 printing / year 98 97 96 95 94

Printed in the United States of America

Contents

"Analyze the gifts of that powerful evangelist as accurately as you can; measure, as closely as may be possible, the secret of his influence; but I do not believe that you will find any other teacher whose printed sermons would be read week after week, year after year, by tens and hundreds of thousands, not only all over England, Scotland, and Wales, but in the backwoods of Canada, on the prairies of America, in the remotest settlements of Australia and New Zealand, wherever an English newspaper can reach, or the English tongue is spoken. The thing is absolutely unique. It has no parallel. . . . What was it that gave [Spurgeon] a religious influence so unparalleled in our day, and made his name a household word all over the wide world? No doubt he had rare gifts. He was courageous, resolute, and lively in these times of the faint heart, irresolution and dullness. He had that genuine eloquence which is all the more effective because of its directness and simplicity. He had a matchless voice, powerful and vibrating with every quality of earnestness and variety. He had humor, tender pathos, and never failed to be interesting. He was utterly untrammelled by the questionings of criticism. But it was, above all, the splendid completeness, the unswerving strength, the exuberant vitality of his faith in God's revelation to man through His Son Jesus Christ, combined with the width and warmth of his zealous love for souls, that gave him that unbounded power which he exercised so loyally for Christian belief. . . ."

Archdeacon Sinclair of St. Paul's Cathedral
on the impact of Spurgeon's ministry

1

*Mary's Magnificat**

And Mary said, My soul doth magnify the Lord, and my spirit hath rejoiced in God my Savior (Luke 1:46–47).

Mary's Magnificat was a song of faith. You have thought, perhaps, that you could easily have sung this song if you had been as highly favored as she was; but are you sure that you could have done so? Have you ever realized the difficulties under which this hymn was composed and sung? If not, permit me to remind you that the wondrous birth, which had been promised to her, had not then been accomplished, and in her mind there must have been a consciousness that many would doubt her statements. The visitation of the angel, and all its consequences, would seem to be ridiculous and even impossible to many to whom she might venture to mention the circumstances; nay, more than that, would subject her to many cruel insinuations, which would scandalize her character, and that which conferred upon her the highest honor that ever fell to woman would, in the judgment of many, bring upon her the greatest possible dishonor. We know what suspicions even Joseph had, and that it was only a revelation from God that could remove them. Mary must have been sorely troubled if she had been influenced by her natural feelings, and had been swayed by external circumstances.

It was only her wondrous faith—in some respects, her matchless faith, for no other woman had ever had such a blessed trial of faith as she had—it was only her matchless faith that she should be the mother of the holy child Jesus, that sustained her. Truly blessed was she in believing that, and blessed indeed was she in that, even before there was an accomplishment of the things that were told her by the angel, she could sing, "My soul doth magnify the Lord, and my spirit hath rejoiced in God my Savior." Unbelief would have said, "Wait." Fear would have said, "Be silent." But

* This sermon was taken from *The Metropolitan Tabernacle Pulpit* and was preached on Thursday evening, April 22, 1875.

faith could not wait, and could not be silent; she must sing, and sing she did most sweetly. I call your attention to this fact because, when we ourselves have a song to sing unto the Lord, we may perhaps be tempted not to sing it until our hopes are accomplished, and our faith has been exchanged for fact. O brother, sister, if this is your case, do not wait, for your song will spoil if you do. There is another song to be sung for the accomplished mercy, but there is a song to be sung now for the promised mercy; therefore, let not the present hour lose the song which is due to it.

I am not going to expound the text so much as to ask you to practice it with me; so, firstly, *let us sing*; secondly, *let us sing after Mary's manner*; and, thirdly, *let us sing with Mary's matter.*

Let Us Sing

LET US SING, first, *because singing is the natural language of joy.* Do not even the ungodly sing when their corn and wine increase? Have they not their harvest hymns and vintage songs? Do they not sing right merrily when they go forth to the dance? And if the wicked sing thus, shall the righteous be silent? Are the jubilant songs all made for the ungodly, and the dirges for us? Are they to lift high the festive strain, and we to be satisfied with the "Dead March" in *Saul*, or some such melancholy music as that? No, brethren, if they have joy, much more have we. Their joy is like the crackling of thorns under a pot; but ours is the shining of a star that never shall be quenched. Let us sing then, for our joy abounds and abides. Therefore, "Rejoice in the Lord alway: and again I say, Rejoice." If the joy of the Lord be your strength, why not express it in holy song? Why should not your joys have a tongue as well as the joys of ungodly men? When warriors win victories, they shout; have we won not victories through Jesus Christ our Lord? When men celebrate their festivals, they sing; are there any festivals equal to ours—our paschal supper, our passage of the Red Sea, our jubilee, our expectation of the coronation of our King, our hymn of victory over all the hosts of hell? Oh, surely, if the children of earth sing, the children of heaven ought to sing far more often, far more loudly, far more harmoniously than they do. Come, then, let us sing because we are glad in the Lord.

Let us sing, too, *because singing is the language of heaven.* It is thus that they express themselves up yonder. Many of the songs and other sounds of earth never penetrate beyond the clouds. Sighs and groans and clamors have never reached those regions of serenity and purity; but they do sing there. Heaven is the home of sacred song, and we are the children of heaven. Heaven's light is in us; heaven's smile is upon us; heaven's all belongs to us; and, therefore—

We would begin the music here,
And so our souls should rise:
Oh, for some heavenly notes to bear
Our passions to the skies!

The music of joy and the music of heaven should often be upon our lips in the form of psalms, and hymns, and spiritual songs.

Let us also sing, *because singing is sweet to the ear of God.* I think I may venture to say that even the song of birds is sweet to Him, for in Psalm 104 where it is written, "The Lord shall rejoice in his works," it is also mentioned that the birds "sing among the branches." Is there anything sweeter in this world than to, wake up, about four or five o'clock in the morning, just at this time of the year, and hear the birds singing as if they would burst their little throats, and pouring out, in a kind of contest of sweetness, their little hearts in joyous song? I believe that, in the wild places of the earth, where no human foot has ever defiled the soil, God loves to walk. When I have been alone among the fir trees, inhaling their sweet fragrance, or have wandered up the hill where the loudest voice could not be answered by another voice for no man was there, I have felt that God was there, and that He loved to listen to the song of birds that He had created. Yes, even the harshly croaking ravens He hears when they cry.

I do not think that mere music is sweet to God's ears when it comes from man in lewdness, attended with lascivious thoughts; and even sacred music, which is sweet in itself, when used for mere amusement, must be an abomination to the Most High when it is so degraded. But He loves to hear us sing when we sing His praises from our hearts. Do you not delight to hear your own children sing, and is there anything sweeter than a song from a child? At the orphanage, the other day, they brought me a little boy who had just been taken in. I felt a special interest in him because his father had been a minister of the gospel. They told him to sing to me, and it was a very sweet song—one of Mr. Sankey's hymns—which came from his lips. His singing quite touched my heart. Had it been my own child, I do not doubt that it would have touched my heart still more; and God loves to hear His children sing. Even your discords, so long as they do not affect your heart, but are only of sound and not of soul, shall please Him. What a beautiful simile is used in Psalm 22: "O thou that inhabitest the praises of Israel!" Just as God's ancient people, during the feast of tabernacles, dwelt under booths made from the boughs of trees, so Jehovah is represented as having made for Himself a tabernacle out of the praises of His people. They are only like fading boughs, that soon turn brown, yet the great Lord of all condescends to sit beneath them; and, as we each one bring a new bough, plucked from the tree of mercy, we help to make a new tabernacle for the Most High to dwell in.

One reason why they sing in heaven is *because all there are seeking to please the heart of God.* They sing not merely that they may practice psalmody, and have their voices in good order, or that they may interest the strangers who are constantly arriving from these nether lands, or even that they may please each other, and delight the angels; but unto the Lord is their perpetual song, for He delights in it. Let us also sing unto Him as long as we live. Sometimes, it would be well for us to make hymns, rather than to repress the making of them, as we often do. The Moravians were accustomed to gather up, in their churches, the very poorest rhymes and ditties that were made by the brethren, and they used to shape them as best they could into something like singable form, and their hymn book has in it a great number of hymns that I should not like to hear you sing; but, for all that, I like the spirit that was in the early Moravians. "Let us each one try to make a hymn," said they. "Let us encourage one another to express some personal experience of our life, for we have each one of us had some special point of God's grace illustrated in us." I would that the men, who can so well write popular songs, and give to the people attractive words and tunes to sing in the street or in the home, would consecrate their talents to a better purpose by writing hymns and spiritual songs to the praise and glory of God. We should then be the richer in our psalmody, as, indeed, we always are when God lends us a true revival of religion, for revivals of religion always bring with them new hymns and spiritual songs.

But if we cannot ourselves compose hymns, let us sing those that somebody else has made, and let us sing the right ones, those that suit us best. There are some hymns that I cannot sing at present; they are too high for me, but I shall sing them by-and-by. There are others that are too low for me; I cannot get down to such depths of doubt and trembling as the poets seem to have been in when they composed them. Every Christian should have some particular hymn that he loves best, so that, when his heart is merriest, he should sing that hymn. How many good old people I have known, who used to sit and sing, or walk about the house, just humming or crooning—

When I can read my title clear
To mansions in the skies,
I bid farewell to every fear,
And wipe my weeping eyes.

Some have other favorites; but, whatever our choice is, I think it is well to have a hymn which, although we have not ourselves written it, has, nevertheless, been made our own by our circumstances and experiences. When we have fixed on such a hymn as that, let us sing it unto the Lord again and again.

Let us not be among those who make excuses for not singing. One says that he has no voice. Then, sing with your heart, brother. Perhaps even your voice would improve if you used it more; but if there be such a grating noise about it that you dare not sing when another person is listening, get alone, and sing unto the Lord.

Do not say that you are unable to sing because you are always in company. I would have you make it your general rule to sing in almost any company where your lot may be cast; though, some times, it is not meet to cast your pearls before swine. Watch your opportunity; if all in the room are silent, perhaps you had better be silent, too; but if one of your work fellows feels that he must needs sing a song, and he has taken the liberty to do it, now is your turn, and you may sing, too. I remember being on mount St. Bernard, spending a night with the monks at the hospice. There was a piano, which had been given by the Prince of Wales, and the different persons who were spending the night there, sang and played by turns. One sang a Spanish hymn, and another a German hymn, and when it came to our turn, we sang—

> There is a fountain filled with blood
> Drawn from Immanuel's veins.

And why should we not sing it? Had we not as good a right to sing as the other people had? Do not you abate your rights and privileges, dear friends; but, if others sing, do you sing, too, and never mind who listens; it will do no man any hurt to hear the praises of the Lord.

And do not say that you cannot sing because of your occupation. Your hands may be just as busy as usual even while the songs of Zion are rising from your lips. You may even be writing, or otherwise mentally occupied, and yet, at the same time, your heart may be ascending to God in praise.

Make no excuse because you are ill. Sometimes, a little song between the sheets is very sweet in the ears of God, even though it has to be accompanied by sighs and groans. Pain makes every note come out with great effort, yet I believe God bends down His ear to hear such singing as that. I have known birds in cages sing better than those outside; and the Lord sometimes puts us in a cage on purpose that He may hear us sing the sweeter. He loves to hear His sick children sing His praises upon their beds, and His high praises in the midst of the furnace of affliction. Are you very poor? Then sing from your heart unto the Lord, and your music shall be better than silver and gold unto God. Even death itself need not stay our songs; let us sing right up to this side of the glory gate, there is no fear about our keeping on with our song on the other side. So long as we can sing here, let us do so, praising the Lord right up to the last hour of our lives, then shall our voices be tuned immediately to nobler songs, for, in a moment, we shall—

Sing with rapture and surprise
His lovingkindness in the skies.

Let Us Sing After Mary's Manner

Now, passing on to our second point, LET US SING AFTER MARY'S MANNER, as far as that manner may be transferable to us. No bird ought to try to sing exactly like another. The blackbird ought not to imitate the thrush, nor the thrush the canary; let them all keep to their own notes, and let each one of us sing his own song unto the Lord. Yet I think we shall see that there is something about Mary's music that will suit us all.

First, *let us sing reverently.* Mary was very joyful, but there was nothing in her song that would strike you as being irreverent, vulgar, or commonplace. I am not squeamish about music, but I must confess that I hardly like to hear the high praises of God sung to the tune of a comic song or of a dance. There is a certain congruity about things that must be observed, and some good music may have associated with it such queer ideas that we had better let it alone till those associations have died out, lest, haply, while we are uttering holy words, some people may be reminded by the tune of unholy things. Mary sings very reverently, and so should we; and though I like some of the new tunes very well, and am glad that they are so popular, yet, for my own part, I like a good old psalm tune much better. It seems to me like going away from the snows of Lebanon to seek after the stale cisterns of earth, when we leave the old music, and the old hymns, and the old psalms, for any of your modern melodies. Still, if you can praise God better with the new songs, do so; but let it always be done reverently.

But, secondly, *Mary praised God with personal devotion.* Notice how intensely personal her song is. Elizabeth is there, yet Mary sings as though she were all alone: "My soul doth magnify the Lord, and my spirit hath rejoiced in God my Savior." It seemed as though her song meant something like this, "Elizabeth is glad, but I, Mary, also am glad, and I have a gladness which is all my own, which even Elizabeth cannot know. 'My soul doth magnify the Lord.'" It ought to be so in our congregations; we should join wide our fellow-Christians in their songs of praise, but we must always mind that our personal note is not omitted, "*My* soul doth magnify the Lord." Do you not think that some of you too often forget this? You come to hear sermons, and sometimes you do not come to the assembly as much as you ought for the purpose of directly and distinctly praising God in your own personality and individuality. The music is delightful to us as it rises from thousands of voices, but to God it can be pleasant only as it comes from each heart. "My soul"—whether other people are praising the Lord or not;—"my soul"—for I have a personal indebtedness to You, my God, and there is a personal union between You and me; I love You, and

You love me; and, therefore, even if all other souls are dumb, "my soul doth magnify the Lord." In this fashion, dear brother or sister, have a song to yourself, and mind that it is thoroughly your own.

Thirdly, *in Mary's song we see great spirituality*. You observe how she puts this matter twice over: "My *soul* doth magnify the Lord, and my *spirit* hath rejoiced in God my Savior." She is far from being content with mere lip service. Her language is poetic, but she is not satisfied with her language. I have no doubt that her voice was exceedingly sweet, but she does not say anything about that, but she does speak of "my soul" and "my spirit." O dear friends, let us never be satisfied with any kind of worship which does not take up the whole of our inner and higher nature. It is what you are within that you really are before the living God; and it is quite a secondary matter how loud the chant may be, or how sweet the tone of your hymn, or how delightfully you join in it, unless your spirit, your soul, truly praises the Lord. You can sometimes do this in "songs without words"; and he that has no voice for singing can, after this fashion, magnify the Lord with his soul and spirit.

Mary also praised the Lord intelligently. Notice how she sings: "My soul doth magnify *the Lord*, and my spirit hath rejoiced in *God my Savior*." You observe that she varies the names which she uses, and she varies them with great propriety. She magnifies Jehovah; she makes Him great; which is the proper thing to do concerning Jehovah; but she rejoices in God her Savior. In that aspect, her Lord comes nearer to her, and becomes more immediately the object of joy to her, so she rejoices in God her Savior. She dwells first upon Jehovah's power to save: "My soul doth magnify *the Lord*." Then she dwells upon His willingness to save: "My spirit hath rejoiced in *God my Savior*." She seems to see the two points—the greatness and the goodness of the Lord; Jehovah, yet her Savior; the Ruler and Lawgiver, yet the gracious One who pardons and blots out sin.

Mary praised God enthusiastically, for the reduplication of the terms, "My soul doth magnify the Lord, and my spirit hath rejoiced in God my Savior," indicates the fervor and ardor of her praise. It is natural to us to repeat ourselves when we begin to glow with holy gladness, so Mary says, "My soul, my natural life—my spirit, my newborn, my intenser, diviner life—my soul, my mind, my intellect—my spirit, my affections, my heart, my emotions, my entire being, my soul and spirit praise the Lord." She did not need to add that her body praised the Lord, for the very sound of her voice bore witness that her body was joining with her soul and spirit, and that so her triple nature was magnifying the Lord. There was enthusiasm in her song; and if ever any of us ought to be stirred to the very depths of our spirit, it is when we are praising the Lord. Sing, brethren, sing sweetly, but sing loudly, too, unto God your strength.

Further, we may sing, as Mary did, *divinely*; I mean, of course, with regard to the object of her song. So let it be with us. "My soul doth magnify the Lord; and my spirit hath rejoiced in"—the success of my pastor's ministry? Yes, it may do so, but that is one of the inferior themes for joy. "My spirit hath rejoiced in" my own success in casting out devils, and working miracles? Ay, it may do that; but, still, it would be better to rejoice that our names are written in heaven. The subject of Mary's joy is nothing low, nothing less than heavenly: "My spirit hath rejoiced in God my Savior." If that is your declaration, you may well lift up your voice and sing—

Go up, go up, my heart,
Dwell with thy God above.

Note, again, that *Mary sang evangelically*, and we must mind that we always do the same, for I am afraid that there are some popular hymns which have something that is not gospel in them; and whenever there is a hymn that has the slightest taint of that sort in it, we ought to abandon it forever, however sweet its poetry may be. Mary sings, "My spirit doth rejoice in God my Savior." She was no Socinian, and she was no Romanist; she knew that she needed a Savior, and that she needed a God for her Savior, so her spirit rejoiced in God her Savior. When we reach the highest point in our devotions, we still need a Savior. I do not at all like the boastful talk about "the higher life" in which some people seem to revel. We cannot have too high a life; but "God be merciful to me a sinner," is about as big a prayer as I can manage at present; and often does my soul pray with such earnestness the dying thief's prayer that his petition is forced to my lips, "Lord, remember me when thou comest into thy kingdom." The place of the perfect does not suit me yet, at any rate, but the place of the publican and of the penitent more becomes me, as I think it does the most of us. Oh, yes! we still need a Savior; so, like Mary, we will sing about our Savior; and even if we walk in the light, as God is in the light, we cannot do without the blood of Jesus Christ constantly cleansing us from all sin, for sin we do still.

Once more, *Mary praised the Lord with assurance*. It is a grand thing to be able to sing, "My soul *doth* magnify the Lord, and my spirit *hath* rejoiced in God"—"who will, I hope, and pray, and sometimes believe, be my Savior"? I have spoiled the music—have I not—by putting in those words of my own? It goes better as Mary sang it, "My spirit hath rejoiced in God my Savior." She was quite assured of that fact, and had not any doubts or fears concerning it. It is well to get such a firm grip of the Savior that we rest in Him completely, and so can sing to His praise. "Oh!" says one, "I cannot praise Jesus as I would, because of my sins"; and I reply to that remark—But, my dear friend, would you praise Him if you had no sins? Would He be needed by you and wanted by you then? Could He be of any use to you then? Would you feel any gratitude to Him? If you were not sinners, of what use would a Savior be to you? But we praise Him because, though we are conscious of sin, we are equally conscious of cleansing in His precious blood. We take Him to be our All-in-all because we ourselves are nothing at all. If we had been of any account, He would have been just so much less; but, since we are nothing, there is the opportunity for Him to be All-in-all to us. Let us sing, then, to His praise; may God the Holy Spirit teach us to do so, even as He taught the Virgin Mary!

Let Us Sing with Mary's Matter

Now, thirdly, and briefly, LET US SING WITH MARY'S MATTER. That was twofold: "My soul doth magnify the Lord, and my spirit hath rejoiced in God my Savior."

The first part of our matter, then, should be, "*Magnify the Lord.*" How can we do that? We cannot really make God great, though that is the meaning of the word. How, then, can we magnify Him?

Well, first, let us think of His greatness; it will be really praising Him if we thus think of Him. You need not speak, but just ponder, weigh, consider, contemplate, meditate, ruminate upon the attributes of the Most High. Begin with His mercy if you cannot begin with His holiness; but take the attributes one by one, and think about them. I do not know a single attribute of God which is not wonderfully quickening and powerful to a true Christian. As you think of any one of them, it will ravish you, and carry you quite away. You will be lost in wonder, love, and praise as you consider it; you will be astonished and amazed as you plunge into its wondrous depths, and everything else will vanish from your vision. That is one way of making God great,—by often thinking about Him.

The next way to make God great is by often drinking Him into yourself. The lilies stand and worship God simply by being beautiful—by drinking in the sunlight which makes them so charming, and the dewdrops which glisten upon them. Stand before the Lord, and drink Him in; do you understand what I mean by this expression? You go down to the seaside, when you are sickly, and you get out on a fine morning, and there is a delightful breeze coming up from the sea, and you feel as if it came in at every pore of your body, and you seem to be drinking in health at every breath you breathe. Do just like that in a spiritual sense with God, go down to the great sea of Godhead; magnify It by thinking how great It is, and then take It into your very soul. God cannot be greater than He is, but He can be greater in you than He is at present. He cannot increase; there cannot be more of God than there is, but there may be more of God in you. More of His great love, more of His perfect holiness, more of His divine power may be manifested in you, and more of His likeness and light may be revealed through you. Therefore, make Him great in that respect.

And when you have done that, by His help, then try to make Him great by what you give forth, even as the rose, when she has satisfied herself with the sweet shower, no sooner does the clear shining come after the rain, than she deluges the garden all around with her delicious perfume. Do you the same; first drink in all you can of the Deity, and then exhale Him; breathe out again, in your praise, in your holy living, in your prayers, in your earnest zeal, in your devout spirit, the God whom you have breathed in. You cannot make more of God than He is, but you can make God more consciously present to the minds of others, and make them think more highly of God by what you say and what you do.

I should like to be able to say, as long as I live, "My soul doth magnify the Lord." I should like to have this as the one motto of my life from this moment until I close my eyes in death, "My soul doth magnify the Lord." I would fain preach that way; I would fain eat and drink that way; I would even sleep that way, so that I could truthfully say, "I have no wish but that God should be great, and that I should help to make Him great in the eyes of others." Will not you also, dear friends, make this the motto of your life-psalm?

Then Mary added, "*and my spirit hath rejoiced in God my Savior.*" Is there any true praise without joy? Is not praise twin brother to joy? And do not joy and praise ever dwell together? Rejoice, then, beloved, not in the scenes you see, for they are fleeting, but rejoice in your Savior—in Him above everything else. Never let any earthly thing or any human being stand higher in your joy than Jesus Christ of Nazareth. Rejoice in Him as most surely yours; for, dear brother, as a believer, Christ is yours. If you are resting in Him, He belongs to you; so rejoice in your own Savior, for all of Christ is yours—not half a Savior; not one of His wounds for you, and one for me; but all His wounds for you, and all for me; not His thoughtful head for you, and His loving heart for me; but His head and His heart all for you and all for me—He is my Savior, from His feet that were pierced by the nails to His head that was crowned with thorns.

Oh, how we ought to rejoice in Him, whatever our union with Him may cost us! Mary did not know what that wondrous visitation would cost her; and it was to cost her much, as Simeon said to her, "Yea, a sword shall pierce through your own soul also"; but even though the sword must go through her soul, it matters not to her, for unto her a child was to be born, unto her a son was to be given, who was to be called "Wonderful, Counselor, the Mighty God, the everlasting Father, the Prince of Peace." So, if the fact that Christ is ours involves the bearing of the cross, we are glad to bear it. It may involve suffering and shame, and a thousand temptations and trials; if it be so, each true believer can say with Mary, "'My spirit hath rejoiced in God my Savior'—in what He is, in what He is to me, in what He is to all His sons, in what He is to poor sinners, in what He is to God, in what He will be when He comes again, and in what He will be throughout eternity." If a little bird has nothing else to do but sing, it has a great deal to do; and if you and I should have, tonight, when we get home, nothing to do but to praise the Lord, we have the best employment out of heaven. We must not think that Christians are wasting time when they pray and praise. Some fussy folk seem to imagine that we must always be talking, or attending meetings, or giving away tracts. Well, do as much as ever you can of all good things; but, still there must be times for quiet meditation, times for reading, times for praying, and times for praising. There is no waste about such times; they are among the best spent hours that we ever have. To work is the stalk of the wheat; but to praise, is the full corn in the ear. You and I, beloved, are the living to praise God. This is the culmination, the very apex of the pyramid of existence, pointing straight up to heaven—that we praise God with all our heart and soul.

So then, to conclude, here is something for every child of God to do. You can all magnify the Lord, and you may all rejoice in Him. You cannot all preach. If you could, who would there be to hear you? If all were preachers, where would be the hearers? But you can all praise God. If there is any brother or sister here who has only one talent, let not such a one say, "I cannot do anything." You can magnify the Lord, and you can rejoice in Him. To be happy in Him is to praise God. The mere fact of our being happy in the Lord makes music in His ears. If you are one of His children, you can be happy in Him, so get out of those doleful dumps; cast out that spirit of murmuring and complaint which so often possesses you. Pray the Lord to help you to shake off your natural tendency to look on the dark side of everything, and say, "No, no; I must not do that. After all, I am not on the road to hell; I am on the way to heaven; and this world is the ante-room to heaven, so my soul shall magnify the Lord, and my spirit shall rejoice in God my Savior." I believe that, if we could brighten the faces of all the saints, and anoint them with the oil of gladness, we should do more than anything else could do to spread Christianity. I mean, if we could make the children of the King rejoice, we should cause worldlings to ask, "Where does this joy come from?" And as they asked this question, we would give them the answer, and so the gospel would be sure to spread.

My closing word is concerning those who cannot magnify the Lord, and cannot rejoice in God their Savior, those who cannot sing to God's praise, and who never have any joy in the Lord. Then, how can they be His children? God has many children, and they have many infirmities; but He never had a dumb child yet. They can every one say, "God be merciful to me a sinner"; and they can all sing, "Worthy is the Lamb that was slain." Prayer and praise are two of the sure signs of a true-born heir of heaven. If you never praise God, my friend, you can never go to heaven. Until the Lord has taken out of you the praise of other things, and the love of other things, and given you the grace to love Himself, and praise Himself, you cannot enter into His glory. May some poor soul here, that has not anything for which it could praise itself, begin now to praise that God who freely forgive the greatest sin, and who is willing to cleanse the very blackest sinner, for He has given Christ to die, the Just for the unjust, that He may bring them unto God. Oh, begin to magnify Him and rejoice in Him now, and you will never want to leave off doing so, world without end. Amen.

2

*Mary Magdalene**

Mary Magdalene, out of whom he had cast seven devils (Mark 16:9).

Experimental preaching, when truthful, is almost always profitable. As the spouse of old desired to see the footsteps of the flock, so souls in distress are always happy to observe the proofs that others have trodden that same pathway heretofore. It may be, and I trust it shall be, that while we are speaking upon the life of Magdalene, and showing how the Lord was pleased to lead her up from the depths of mental distress to the heights of spiritual joy, some who may be in like circumstances may be led to hope that for them also there may be deliverance, and others who have already received like favors, may have their grateful recollections refreshed, and may be made to bless the Lord who aforetime brought them up out of the horrible pit and out of the miry clay, and has now set their feet upon a rock. We shall begin with Mary of Magdala where God began with her, in a way of effectual grace.

A Melancholy Instance of Satanic Power

Mary Magdalene furnishes us, in the first place, with A MELANCHOLY INSTANCE OF SATANIC POWER.

She does not appear to have been a great sinner; it is scarcely possible, and certainly very improbable, that she could have been a transgressor in the sense in which the term "Magdalene" is generally understood. Custom has attached the title of Magdalene to those who have forfeited their good name by open sins against the seventh commandment. Mistaken though it be, let the name always remain as the sole treasure of fallen women, for, if we can give them one honorable designation to act as a shield, pray let them have it, for the world is cold enough and scornful enough toward such offenders. It is worthwhile, however, to declare for the

---

* This sermon was taken from *The Metropolitan Tabernacle Pulpit* and was preached on Sunday morning, January 26, 1868.

honor of Mary Magdalene, that she was no Magdalene in the modern sense; it could scarcely have been so, she was probably a raving demoniac, therefore not at all likely to fall into the sins of the flesh. We are never told of her that she was a great sinner; in fact, not a word is said against her personal character; we are simply informed that she was possessed with seven devils, which is an affliction rather than a crime. I do not deny that sin may have prepared her for the satanic possession, and was no doubt also occasioned by it, but she is not brought before us in Scripture as a transgressor, nor is she the representative of great offenders, but rather the type of a class of persons who for years are sore vexed in heart, greatly depressed in spirit, heavily burdened with despondency, bound with chains of melancholy, subject to distracting forebodings, to alarms of coming wrath, and to a despair unsufferable.

Mary Magdalene represents those who have come under the tormenting and distracting power of Satan, and whose lamp of joy is quenched in tenfold night. They are imprisoned not so much in the dens of sin as in the dungeons of sorrow, not so criminal as they are wretched, not so depraved as they are desolate. We do not with any certainty understand the precise nature of being possessed with the devil. Holy Scripture has not been pleased to acquaint us with the philosophy of possessions, but we know what the outward symptoms were. Persons possessed with devils were unhappy; they found the gloom of the sepulcher to be their most congenial resort. They were unsocial and solitary. If they were permitted, they broke away from all those dear associations of the family circle which give half the charms to life: they delighted to wander in dry places, seeking rest and finding none: they were pictures of misery, images of woe. Such was the seven times unhappy Magdalene, for into her there had entered a complete band of devils. She was overwhelmed with seven seas of agony, loaded with seven manacles of despair, encircled with seven walls of fire. Neither day nor night afforded her rest, her brain was on fire, and her soul foamed like a boiling caldron. Miserable soul! No dove of hope brought the olive branch of peace to her forlorn spirit, she sat in the darkness and saw no light—her dwelling was in the valley of the shadow of death. Among all the women of Magdala there was none more wretched than she, the unhappy victim of restless and malicious demons. Those who were possessed with these evil spirits, were defiled thereby, as well as made unhappy; for a heart cannot become a kennel for the hounds of hell without being rendered filthy and polluted. I suppose that in addition to the natural corruptions which would be in Mary as well as in ourselves, there would be a more than human nimbleness to evil, a vivacity, an outspokenness about all her sinful propensities, which only the indwelling fiend could give. Satan being within, would be sure to stir up the coals of impure thoughts and evil desires, so that the fire of sin would burn vehemently.

Her inner self may have been sorely troubled with such excess of wickedness, but she was without power to damp the furnace of her mind. She would be incessantly assaulted by unearthly profanities and hideous suggestions; not as with us, proceeding from the devil without, who is a dreaded antagonist, but from seven devils within, who had entrenched themselves upon a dreadful vantage ground. She was in that sense, no doubt, greatly polluted, although it would be difficult to say how far she was accountable for it, on account of the dislodgment of her reason. In addition to the unhappiness and the defilement occasioned by Satanic possession, these persons were frequently dangerous to others and to themselves. Sometimes, we read, they were cast into the fire, and anon into the water; some cut themselves with knives or sharp stones, others tore their garments in pieces, and even when bound in chains—according to the old fashioned method of controlling lunatics—they burst their bonds. Such persons must have been very undesirable inmates of any house, however remote their chamber. It must frequently have been necessary to confine them apart, for in their madness they were not to be trusted; for, as is often the case, those who had been nearest and dearest to them, became the first objects of their enmity. To give a spiritual turn to the subject, let me remark that it is one of the most dreadful things about some of those who are plunged in unbelief, that the mischief of their misery is not confined to themselves, but extends to their families and connections. Their example drips like the upas tree, with poison; they are like the clouds that gathered over Sodom, full of fiery hail; they bring sadness and sorrow wherever their influence is felt. The man who has laid in beds of spices, spreads perfume on all sides; but the man who has familiar intercourse with horrors, like one fresh come from the lazar house, bears all the seeds of death about him in the gloom and melancholy which he spreads abroad. To sum up much in a few words, there is no doubt that Mary Magdalene would have been considered by us to be demented—she was, practically, a maniac. Reason was unshipped, and Satan stood at the helm instead of reason, and the poor barque was hurried hither and thither under the guidance of demons. What a dreadful state to be in! And yet, dear friends, though actual Satanic possession is unknown among us now, we have seen several cases extremely like it, and we know at this hour some who baffle altogether all attempts to comfort them, and make us feel that only the good Physician can give them rest. I remember a man of excellent character, well beloved by his family and esteemed by his neighbors, who was for twenty years enveloped in unutterable gloom. He ceased to attend the house of God, because he said it was of no use; and although always ready to help in every good word and work, yet he had an abiding conviction upon him that, personally, he had no part nor lot in this matter, and never could have. The more you talked to him, the worse he became; even prayer seemed but to excite him to more fearful despondency. In the providence of God I was called to preach the Word in his neighborhood; he was induced to attend, and, by God's gracious power, under the sermon he obtained a joyful liberty. After twenty years of anguish and unrest, he ended his weary roamings at the foot of the cross, to the amazement of his neighbors, the joy of his household, and the glory of God. Nor did his peace of mind subside, for until the Lord gave him a happy admission into eternal rest, he remained a vigorous believer, trusting and not being afraid. Others are around us for whom we earnestly pray that they also may be brought out of prison to praise the name of the Lord.

Magdalene's case was a perfectly helpless one; men could do nothing for her. All the surgery and physic in the world would have been wasted upon her singular malady. Had it been any form of physical disease or purely mental derangement, help might have been attainable, but who is a match for the crafty and cruel fiends of the pit? No drugs can lull them to sleep, no knife can tear them from the soul. The loving friend and the skillful adviser stood equally powerless, nonplussed, bewildered, dismayed. Mary was in a hopeless condition. There was nothing known by any, even the wise men of the east, of any method by which seven evil spirits could be dislodged. However expensive the remedy, her relatives would have resorted to it; but who can cope with devils? Doubtless all who knew her thought that death would be a great relief to her, and would relieve her family of wearisome anxiety and fear. Although willing to help, they could not aid in the slightest degree, and had the hourly sorrow of seeing her endure an agony which they could not alleviate. Magdalene was the victim of Satanic influence in a most fearful form: sevenfold were the spirits which possessed her; and there are men and women nowadays who are tempted by the great enemy of souls to a most awful degree. Some of us have endured temporary seasons of frightful depression, which have qualified us to sympathize with those who are more constantly lashed by the fury of the infernal powers. We too have had our horror of great darkness. We have groaned with David, "I am troubled; I am bowed down greatly; I go mourning all the day long. . . . I am feeble and sore broken: I have roared by reason of the disquietness of my heart. . . . My heart panteth, my strength faileth me: as for the light of mine eyes, it also is gone from me." We have been, though only for a few days or hours at a time, reduced to such an utter prostration of heart, that our soul chose strangling rather than life, for the sorrows of death compassed us, and the pains of hell gat hold upon us—we found trouble and sorrow. Believe me, brethren, this is no child's play, but a thing to turn the hair gray, and plow deep furrows on the brow. It is no trivial sorrow to lament with the weeping prophet. "Is it nothing to you, all ye that pass by? behold, and see if there be any sorrow like unto my sorrow, which is done unto me, wherewith the Lord hath afflicted me in the day of his fierce anger. From above hath he sent fire into my bones, and it prevaileth against them: he hath spread a net for my feet, he hath turned me back: he hath made me desolate and faint all the day. The yoke of my transgressions is bound by his hand: they are wreathed, and come up upon my neck: he hath made my strength to fall, the Lord hath delivered me into their hands, from whom I am not able to rise up."

It is a melancholy fact that some persons continue for months and years to drink this cup of trembling. John Bunyan's case is to the point, for he floundered in the Slough of Despond as long as any of the pilgrims whom he has so graphically described. In his instance, those succeeding shadows, those variations of unbelief, those recurring glooms all arose from the same fruitful source of ill: Satan was afraid that he was about to lose a bondslave, and therefore aroused himself to prevent his captive's escape. Like the city of Mansoul when besieged by the troops of Immanuel, when Diabolus was loath to leave, the evil one barricades the doors, and strengthens the walls, so that there may be no entrance for the word of truth. Moreover, as we are told in the Revelation, the devil has great wrath when he knows that his time is short; and he takes care, like a bad tenant, to do all the mischief he can before he is ejected. I may be addressing some such persons here, or in after days my words may meet the eye of poor tortured souls, O that they might find rest! It Is painful in the extreme to meet with such unhappy minds, they are the great difficulty of a pastor's work; so great indeed is the difficulty, that workers with little faith are ready to give up the task, and to leave the matter as impracticable. We have known those who have felt that they could pray no longer for their inconsolable friends: verily, beloved, we must not yield to so heartless a suggestion. As we said the other Sabbath morning, until the gate of hell is shut upon a man, we must not cease to pray for him; and if we see him hugging the very door posts of damnation, we must go to the mercy seat and beseech the arm of grace to pluck him from his dangerous position. While there is life there is hope, and, although the soul is almost smothered with despair, we must not despair for it, but rather arouse ourselves to awaken the almighty arm. The case of the Magdalene is a looking glass in which many souls wrung with anguish may see themselves.

A Glorious Trophy of Diviner Grace

Secondly, Mary Magdalene became A GLORIOUS TROPHY OF DIVINER GRACE.

She is described in the text as "Mary Magdalene, out of whom he had cast seven devils." Sovereign grace is resplendent in Mary's history; in the first place, because this cure was *unsought by her*. Others who were sick sought the healing hand of Jesus, but no person possessed of an evil spirit ever did or ever could cry for deliverance to the Son of David: their friends might bring them, but they never came of themselves. The evil spirit drives men as far as possible away from Christ, and clamors against Jesus as a tormentor; but it never guides men into the pathway of the merciful Savior. Even thus is it with us all, and especially with desponding souls. If we are saved, it is not because we have the first motions of desire toward Christ, but because eternal love casts its cords around us, and draws us toward the Lord Jesus. There may be disputes about this as matter of doctrine, but I do not believe it can be questioned as a fact in experience. All believers unite in the song—

> Jesus sought me when a stranger,
> Wandering from the fold of God.

We all feel that, if we are converted, the power which turned us is from above.

> 'Tis not that I did choose thee,
> For, Lord, that could not be;
> This heart would still refuse thee,
> But thou hast chosen me:
> Thou from the sin that stain'd me
> Washed me and set me free,
> And to this end ordain'd me,
> That I should live to thee.

If we have repented, our repentance was not a plant indigenous to the barren soil of our corrupt hearts—the seed of it was sown within by a gracious hand. If we have believed in Jesus, our faith was not fashioned on our own anvil, but bestowed upon us from the armory of God. Faith is as much the gift of God as salvation itself. Brethren, we cannot, in our own cases, do otherwise than ascribe all the glory to sovereign grace. "Ye have not chosen me, but I have chosen you." "I am found of them that sought me not." No sinner is beforehand with God, but God's prevenient grace outruns the sinner's first desire; yea, grace come to dead souls when as yet they are not capable of a right emotion. Mary's case, as it illustrates this principle, may help us to see clearly the great love wherewith Jesus loved us, even when we were dead in sins. Poor trembling soul, Jesus can come to you if you cannot come to Him. If your miseries have shut *you* up, they cannot shut *Him* out. Your extremity is God's opportunity, therefore be of good cheer.

It is most likely that Mary *resisted* the healing hand, for so it was with other demoniacs: "What have we to do with thee, Jesus, thou son of God?" The devil was no sooner aware of Christ's presence, than he began to cry out against his Conqueror. If it was not so with Mary, it certainly is so with us, and especially with the subjects of despair. How we resisted conscience! We used what means we could to strangle it, so that its cries might not alarm us. How we labored to quench the Holy Spirit! We had no heart to leave the ways of flesh-pleasing lust, we held to our iniquities as the leech to the flesh. We were willing to run all risks of hell, and lose the glories of heaven. We chose our delusions and hugged our destructions; we were in darkness, and we loved darkness rather than light, because our deeds were evil. Our corrupt heart was enmity against God, and was not reconciled to Him, neither indeed could it be. Strange to say, despair is often voluntary, and men resolve to remain in it, being as fond of the prison as the poor wretch who after years of confinement found liberty to be a pain. Like David's fool, we abhor all manner of meat, though dying for want of it; we blow out the candles lest we should see the light; and contend with the mercy which comes to our rescue. Great Lord! What a madman a sinner is! How irrational are those who pine in despondency, and yet thrust hope away with both their hands. It is a hard task for the surgeon when his patient tears open the veins which he labors to bind up. His skill must be great if he can heal a patient who struggles in his arms, and refuses his affectionate care. Brethren, since in a measure, we have all acted thus, let us admire the dear patience and precious love which bore with our ill manners, and would not let us die! How shall we magnify sufficiently effectual grace, which without violating the freedom of our will, led our captivity captive, making us willing in the day of His power. Let the highest and sweetest notes of all believing psalmody be to omnipotent grace, which wrought in us according to the working of His mighty power, which He wrought in Christ when He raised Him from the dead, and set Him at His own right hand. Glory be to God, though a legion of devils possessed the heart, the power of Jesus is able to cast them out of him, ay, and to set aside the present mad unwillingness which makes the sinner despise his own mercy and hasten to his own ruin.

Those possessed with devils were healed *by a word* from Jesus. Beloved, if we have been saved, the instrument which the Holy Spirit used was the Word, either read in private or heard from the lip of God's minister. "He sent his word and healed them." The Word is the living and incorruptible seed. The ordinance of preaching can scarcely be too much prized, for "it has pleased God by the foolishness of preaching to save them that believe." "For the preaching of the cross is to them that perish foolishness; but unto us which are saved it is the power of God." You who are desponding, I pray you, do not forsake the gathering of yourselves together; although despair may hang about you, still resort to the place where the word is dispensed, and ere long like that daughter of Abraham, whom Satan had bound for eighteen years, who yet went up to the synagogue, you shall, like her, be made whole. While the Word of God is within your reach, there may yet be a love-word for you, even for you. While earnest lips are telling out the love of Jesus, wait with the hope that as the small rain drops upon the tender herb, grace may drop lovingly upon you. "Faith cometh by hearing." Why may it not come to you? The Lord, whom you seek, will suddenly come in His temple; He may tarry, but to every sincere seeker His coming is sure.

She was healed instantaneously, for the cures of our Lord were always such. He said, "Come out of her," to the unclean spirit, and out came the spirit without delay; so that in a single moment, poor demoniac Mary was made to sit at Jesus' feet in peace, and in her right mind. My brethren, what a change it must have been for her! Her soul had been like the lake of Galilee when lashed with the storm: but Christ had said, "Peace, be still," and now there was a great calm. She had been ready to tear herself and hurt others, but now she was obedient to the Master's command, and ministered to Him with joy; she drank in the words of truth, and told them out to others: defiling influences were cast out of her, and she sought after holiness. Had you met her after her cure, you would not have known her to be the same woman. Those disheveled locks no longer remained to betoken the maniac, and those straining eyes and that tortured brow, and all the air and mien of one distraught—all these were changed. She was admitted into society as a reasonable being; she was taken into the family circle as a welcome inmate—Jesus became her teacher, and His apostles her friends. What a miracle of love! Let us entertain hope for our friends in their worst estate, that the like may happen to them. Perhaps God may permit some of His people to fall into this desperate condition, that He may exhibit illustrious instances of what conversion can do. In heaven there is joy over a sinner's repentance: angels do not rejoice in extraordinary conversions merely, but "over one sinner that repenteth"; still, as far as you and I are concerned, when we sit at church meetings and hear of cases of conversion, the more remarkable ones give us greatest joy. When we hear of a sinner brought to Christ, or of another being comforted who had been in dreadful depression of spirit, we are all filled with wonder and delight. It sheds a luster over the Lord's work, and acts like a tonic to our spirits, it refreshes the doubting ones, and those who had become dispirited in service, take courage and say, "We shall never doubt again, for after such an instance as this, we must believe that all things are possible with God." I think the Lord suffers these Magdalenes to be here and there discovered that they may be proof to all the world that He can do whatsoever He wills, and that none are beyond His power. Do I address one who is in such a state? I cannot pass on without the hope that such a troubled mind may speedily look to Jesus. Friend, He can heal you. I know the devil within you says, "You are cast out forever." but Satan is the father of lies, therefore care not for his suggestions. Did you notice how the text declares that Jesus *cast out* the seven devils? The evil ones did not go out of themselves; Magdalene did not drive them out, but *Jesus cast* them out with force and power. The evil one is strong, but Christ is stronger than he, and drives him out speedily when he comes to claim dominion. "Ah," say you, "if he ever gets the devil out of me, I will praise Him." That's the very reason why I think He will do it, in order that He may win your heart, and make you, as long as you live, to wonder, and adore, and admire.

An Ardent Follower of Christ

After she had thus obtained her healing, she became AN ARDENT FOLLOWER OF CHRIST.

We are informed by Mark and Luke, that Mary Magdalene and other holy women followed Jesus into Galilee upon His memorable preaching tour; and when He came up from Galilee to Jerusalem, we find Mary still at the head of that blessed company. I suppose that she had no family, most probably no children, and that her relatives may have come to feel as if she was not one of themselves at all, through her having been so long possessed. She probably possessed some small landed property which yielded her sufficient for her wants. When she was restored, her friends, though exceedingly glad to hear it, might feel as if she had never been one of the family, and therefore did not wish her to return to them, especially when she had become a Christian. Everything leads us to suppose that she had no one near who claimed her personal care, and having a little income, she resolved to devote her life to listening to the Man who had delivered her from her terrible disease. A wise resolve. Happy was she to be allowed to hear His gracious words and see His mighty deeds. She not only listened to Him, but she followed Him. Whoever might turn away, the Magdalene was always close at His side. Through floods and flames, if He was pleased to lead, she had resolved to go. In addition to this, we are told that she ministered unto Him of her substance. That bag which Judas carried, would always have been empty had it not been for this woman of Magdala, and for the wife of Herod's steward (and perhaps Martha, and Mary, and Lazarus), but these generous hearts, knowing that the laborer is worthy of his hire, were glad to contribute of their temporal goods to Him who so greatly enriched them in spiritual things. So Magdalene gave herself, her ear, her foot, her heart, her substance, her all to Jesus. It was not an unusual thing in the Jewish nation for great rabbis to be followed both by men and women in their tours of instruction throughout the country, so that she was not outraging the customs of her people. No doubt our Lord would have said to Mary, "Go home to your friends," if duty required her there, but as she had no other duties to demand her attention, she was allowed to give up all her time to sacred study and to hallowed service. Now, it is not desirable that you or I should leave our kindred and forsake our vocations, but we can nevertheless abide with Jesus as closely as the Magdalene. If we have been delivered from great sin or from great despair, should we not say in our souls, "Now, from this day I will be the constant student of Jesus

Christ's teaching. The gospel has done so much for me that I will seek to know all of it that can be known this side the grave. I will pry into its mysteries, press into its spiritualities, and learn its precepts. And while I am a learner I will also be a follower. Where Christ is I will go. His example shall be law to me. I will pray to have His Spirit. I will ask to be conformed to His image, and what the Master was, that shall the servant be. I will give to Him of my substance. If I can, I will give much, but if I have not much, I will give in fair proportion. I will make a system of offering to God: He shall have a set portion of all my income, and that I will put aside, so that when there is a call for it, I shall not imagine that I am giving from my own purse, but I will give my Lord's money, which has already been consecrated. Then I shall not feel as if I were giving, but as if I were only a steward, handing out what belonged to Christ before? Where persons love little, do little, and give little, we may shrewdly suspect that they have never had much affliction of heart for their sins and that they think they owe but very little to divine grace. He who has received much, if his heart be right, is sure to give much to the Lord, and to say—

And if I might make some reserve,
And duty did not call,
I love my God with zeal so great
That I would give him all.

Behold and admire the difference between the poor demoniac and the faithful follower of Christ—the woman possessed with seven devils, and now the honorable Christian woman ministering unto the Lord of angels! What cannot grace do? No doubt, Mary of Magdala had to suffer much in thus following Christ, for all the disciples had to partake in Christ's cross. They were all thought to be madmen and fools in taking up with the Man of Nazareth, but we never read that Mary shrank. "From that time many went back, and walked no more with him," but Magdalene was true. Again we read, "Many were offended at him because of this saying," but we find not that the woman of Magdala was offended. She held to her Lord in holy faith. She knew the Shepherd's voice, and she followed Him whithersoever He might be please to lead. Happy are those who from their earliest days have been led to see their indebtedness to Christ, and are now resolved to cleave to Him, to serve Him with heart, and soul, and strength, to sit at His feet to catch His words, and then to go abroad and practice what they have learned! I wish we could all attain to a high state of spirituality that we were more strict in our obedience, more close in our communion, more consecrated in our actions. Perhaps it is because we think we have had little forgiven, or owe but little, that therefore we are such little doers and little lovers. Holy Spirit, out of the great sinners of this wicked city, out of the midst of horrible blasphemers, or out of the midst of those who are far gone in horrible despair, call men and women who shall become enthusiasts, flaming with vehement devotion to the Lord.

Faithful Adherent to Her Master Under Trial

Magdalene appears to us farther on in Scripture as a FAITHFUL ADHERENT TO HER MASTER UNDER TRIAL.

It was a dark day for the disciples when Christ was crucified, amid mocking and jeering enemies. We are told by Mark, that Magdalene and Mary, the wife of Cleophas, stood afar off and watched our Lord; but we are informed by John that, among others, there stood at the foot of the cross, Mary Magdalene. I suppose that at the first, when our Lord was nailed to the tree, the disciples could not get into the inner ring, the priests and the Jews were so mad, and the Roman soldiers were so rough, that a woman, however brave, might not venture there. Therefore, as they could not do what they would, they did what they could; they stood at a distance and sobbed and sighed, until their eyes were red, and their hearts were swollen with anguish at the sad sight of Him whom they loved mocked and despised, and shamefully put to death. But by-and-by the crowd grew tired of their cruel amusement, and suddenly there was a darkness over all the land—and it may be that then these timid doves mustered courage and flew to the foot of the tree, passed unnoticed through the soldiers and the crowd, and stood at His feet, and though they could not help Him on the cross, yet they could rally round His cross. If they must not feel the nails, and bleed as He did, yet their hearts were bleeding, and the nails went through their souls. Where was Peter? Where was James? Philip, and Andrew, and Nathanael, where were they? I do not know, but I know where Magdalene was; she was at the tree of doom there, hard by her Lord, glad to confess a persecuted Christ. Here is the test of true love. To follow Christ in peaceful times is easy, but to follow hard after Him when He is despised and rejected of men—here is the pinch. Ah, some of you young people confess to be Christians when you are with Christian people, but will you bear it when your companions sneer at you as a cant and a hypocrite? Can you follow your Lord? Can you follow your Lord when the many turn aside? Can you witness that He has the living Word, and none upon earth beside? Can you stand to Him when you have to suffer loss and reproach, and when His name is the drunkard's song and the fool's proverb? If you can, then blessed be the grace that has taught you to practice so hard a lesson. If there be any who can do this readily, surely they are such as once passed through the deepest waters of soul trouble.

We find Mary last at the sepulcher, viewing the place where the body was laid, and how it was laid; and they spent the evening until the Sabbath hour approached in preparing the spices; then they rested, like devout women, upon the seventh day. It was deep love that made the Magdalene follow the corpse of the Well-beloved right to the tomb. Of that lifeless body every limb was dear to her. He had wrought so great a thing in her, that she could not but feel her heart melt at the thought of His corpse being treated with disrespect. She must see whether they laid it tenderly, whether they put it into its rest with gentleness and honor. She was first at the sepulcher, and was the first to whom Christ appeared. She was faithful to the end. She won the commendation of those of whom it is said, "He that endureth to the end, the same shall be saved."

Be it yours and mine, my brethren, to cling to the truth, even though, like Elijah, we have to say, "I, only I, am left, and they seek my life, to take it away." To keep to a dead cause and an expiring church, to cling to Christ when His cause is rolled in mire, to be ready to be drowned with Christ, to sink with Christ, and rise with Christ, this is genuine affection. This was the Magdalene's love, and let it be ours.

Another sorrow afflicted her after the death of her Lord: it was the fact that the Lord was lost to her. She would have had some melancholy satisfaction if she could have found His body, but in the morning she came to the tomb and found it empty. The beloved body was gone. She wept as one utterly inconsolable. Angels spoke to her, but what were the angels to her—she wanted *Him!* They would have cheered her, but she turned her back: she cared for nothing but her Lord. Those who can worship angels have not Magdalene's spirit, for she turned her back on them. For Christ she sighed. She must have Him or die. You and I may expect times when Jesus will be hidden from us. If we love Him much, we shall weep till we see Him again. They who can rejoice when Christ is absent, have little of His love in their hearts. For where the beams of the Sun of Righteousness are not at the full, there ought to be a winter in the soul. We should sigh and cry until our Lord withdraws the veil, crying out in our hearts, "O that I knew where I might find Him, that I might come even to His seat!"

It is a fine point in Magdalene that she knew how to persevere. She continued to wait and to watch, and while John and Peter had gone home and could be satisfied without seeing Christ, she could not: she must see her Lord. The whole earth could not compose her mind, nor heaven's angels give her comfort until she saw Him whom her soul loved. O heart, are you hungering and thirsting after Him? You shall be well satisfied; meanwhile, count it a great honor thus to hunger and thirst, for you would not do so if you had not loved Him and received much at His hands.

One of the Most Favored Beholders of Christ

I must conduct you one step further. This woman became ONE OF THE MOST FAVORED BEHOLDERS OF CHRIST, for while she sighed and wept, Jesus revealed Himself to her; and after this manner was the revelation—He called her by her name, "Mary."

It has always been thought to be a high distinction when God has called a man by His name. When He spoke and said, "Moses, Moses"; then it was a sign that he had found favor in His sight. When Jesus said, "Mary," I can imagine that the word brought up all her history before her mind; her demoniac days, when her distracted mind was tossed on fiery billows; her happy days, when she sat at her Master's feet and caught His blessed words; the times when she had seen His miracles and wondered; when she had given Him of her substance, and been too glad to minister unto Him. If we love Jesus much, and cannot be content without Him, we too may expect to hear Him in the secret of our soul, calling us by our name. He will say, "I have called thee by thy name: thou art mine." Then Mary Magdalene had such a manifestation of Christ's glory as no other woman ever had. It has been beautifully remarked by one of our dear brethren in the ministry,[1] that that expression, "Touch me not," shows to us that Mary had gone farther in communion than most of us ever think of going, because, she had drawn as near to Jesus as she might be allowed to go. Jesus said, "Touch me not." You and I need not be afraid of His saying that to us: we do not make it necessary. We are at such a distance that He had need to say, "Come near, and nearer still"; but as for Mary, her heart was so knit to Christ, that she approached so near to Him in love, that the Lord knew she could not bear any more, and that her higher joys must be reserved for a higher sphere, and therefore He bade her pause. Besides, He would have her know that He was her Lord and Master as well as her Friend. Affection must not degenerate into familiarity: He must be reverenced as well as loved. Very different was His dealing with Thomas. He commands him to touch. Thomas is such a weak thing, he wants that help, but Mary does not need it; her heart is knit to Him—it leaps for joy—and Jesus having given her as much joy as she could hold, stays her hand. Surely she was like good Mr. Walsh, who said when he was full of the Lord's presence, "Hold, Lord! Remember I am an earthen vessel, and if you give me more I shall die, therefore stay Your loving hand." So was it in the case of Mary. She had very near, and dear, and intimate intercourse with her Master, because she had followed Him and kept close to Him all the days of her life.

An Honored Messenger of Christ to the Apostles

Lastly, Mary became AN HONORED MESSENGER OF CHRIST TO THE APOSTLES.

I feel it no small privilege to be the means of bearing God's message to this congregation. It pleases me when I know that many gray-headed believers, who know far more of experimental truth than I can be supposed to know, have nevertheless been comforted by the message which my Master has sent to them by me. But what an honor to have a message to the

1. Rev. Moody Stuart, to whose book, entitled *The Three Maries*, we refer our readers.

apostles! Oh, the power of grace! Mary, once a demoniac, becomes a preacher to preachers! I dub her Doctor of Divinity indeed, for she has to instruct these mightiest of messengers in the faith.

Note the message. Did ever man preach a better sermon than this woman preached? Had ever minister a more weighty text than this Magdalene had to handle—"I ascend unto my Father and your Father, and to my God and your God"? Angels told of the incarnation, but Magdalene told of the resurrection. She must be made to do alone what a company of angels had been made to do before, to proclaim another step in the Savior's pathway to redemption. My dear friends, you who are so low and distressed this morning, does not this history of Magdalene make you feel like Mercy in the *Pilgrim's Progress*, who laughed in her sleep? Christiana said, "Why did you laugh?" She replied, "Because of my dream." Does not it make your heart leap to think that you—*that you* may one day teach Christ to some of the greatest of His saints; that you a poor distracted wretch on the very brink of hell, may yet see Jesus over and above what others ever see of Him, and may be able to tell to angels, and principalities, and powers, what you have tasted and handled of the good Word of God. Surely, this should breathe hope in you. If you have known my Master, any of you, and have been saved by Him, continue to keep close to Him. If you lose His company, sigh after it, but when you find Him again, make it your delightful business to tell His brethren that He has returned to you, and make their hearts glad as the Lord Jesus has made yours. I shall leave the matter in the hands of the Holy Spirit. May the Lord raise many a Mary Magdalene in the midst of this church, for His name's sake. Amen.

3

*The Water of Life**

The woman saith unto him, Sir, give me this water (John 4:15).

You will remember that our Savior had been speaking to the woman of Samaria concerning living water. He had endeavored to catch her attention by using a metaphor to her work and her position. Water was uppermost in her thoughts, and Jesus sanctified the element to His own gracious end. Sitting at the well's mouth, I think I can see His earnest face, and note the woman's wondering eyes while He talked to her as she had never been spoken to before, concerning water which caused a man never to thirst again. At first the woman raised questions: the skeptical part of her nature took its turn, and caviled, and carped, and argued. "Sir, thou hast nothing to draw with, and the well is deep," and so on. Do you not see all the elements of the infidel in her? But she is in good hands, and soon she has passed from the period of questioning into that of petitioning, and she cries this time, "Sir, give me this water." She was still, I am afraid, very ignorant. She did not even understand her own petition. That is clear from the words which follow the text, "That I thirst not, neither come hither to draw." She was giving a material meaning to a spiritual utterance. She was thinking of the water that could moisten the lips, when Christ was speaking of that living water, His own grace and love, which touches the heart, and the heart only. Her eyes were dark, but her face was turned the right way; and, best of all, Jesus was there, who can lead the blind in a way which they know not. It will be all well with her, you may leave her alone, and think of yourselves.

I hope I am now conversing with some here who have got clear of this woman's ignorance, and have passed away also, as she did, from the period of questioning; you know best who you are and where you are, but I hope you are desirous to partake of the grace which saves. You have got away from raising difficulties. You have had enough of that unprofitable hair-

* This sermon was preached at the Metropolitan Tabernacle, Newington, in 1867.

splitting and cobweb-making. You feel that you get no good by constantly insinuating doubts as to the possibility of your salvation, and questioning whether Christ is a Savior or not, and so you are about to leave the skeptical business, and try another line of things. You are now arrived at the point of desiring, not, I hope, the terminus of the line, but only the first or second station. Glad I am that you have come so far. If there be grace to be had, you are saying, "O that I might have it!" If there be pardon, peace, eternal life, you believe all that Jesus Christ says of it, and you want to possess it. You are stretching out your hands, like the drowning man who is ready to catch at the plank. Your desires are awake; your better thoughts are no longer slumbering. You have broken away from indifference and obstinacy, and you are now anxious and desirous to obtain salvation by Jesus Christ.

It is to you that I wish to speak this evening, and I shall first take the text, *and try to use it to excite your desire still further by a description of the water spoken of in the text*; secondly, I shall *try to assure your hearts by some remarks upon the likelihood of your obtaining this water*; and then we shall close *by urging you not to leave this house until the prayer has been requested in heaven, "Lord, give me this water; give me this water tonight!"*

A Description of the Water Spoken

To begin, then, I am TO TRY TO EXCITE YOUR DESIRE BY A DESCRIPTION OF THE WATER SPOKEN OF IN THE TEXT.

Water is an essential element in the natural world. There is a spiritual world, in describing which, we are obliged to use analogies taken from the natural world; and the grace of God in the mental and the spiritual world, is just what water is in the natural world. You want water as a man; you must have it; on certain occasions it becomes an imperative necessity: you must drink or die. You want grace as a man, not for your body, but for your soul, and it is imperative that you should have it, or else your soul will first be in pain here, and at death the pangs of remorse will seize it, and afterward an everlasting thirst, an unsatisfied want, will be the second death to you.

The grace of God is like water in no less than eight senses. But let me not alarm you. I will not weary you; be sure of that, for I long to win you, and weariness will not serve my purpose. I shall only mention the eight parallels with a few remarks, and pass rapidly on from each one.

1. Water, first, *is thirst-removing*, and so is the grace of God. The man who drinks water, thirsts not, his bodily want is removed; the man who receives the grace of God in his heart, gets that which his nature is wanting, and his painful longings are over. Man by nature is so foolish that he does not know what his nature wants, but he feels that it wants something. Awakened men talk to themselves in this fashion, "I want—I do not know

what I want—but I know I want something which the world cannot give me, which I cannot find within myself, which my fellow men cannot bestow upon me; I want a something: O my God, what is it? Tell me what it is!" Friend, if you are in this condition, the gospel of our Lord Jesus Christ is just the thing for you, for in it the Lord not only tells you what you want, but He presents it to you. He tells you that you need His love; that if His grace be shed abroad in your heart, and your sin be pardoned, and you be made to be His child, and accepted through Christ Jesus, then will your soul say, "Now I have what I wanted; now I want no more; I can sit still and say, Blessed be God that my desires are full. The aching void which the world could never fill is now filled to overflowing; and my soul has what it was always wanting, though it did not know what it really wanted. I can sit down now perfectly content!" It is a grand thing for a man to be able to say, "I am satisfied," but the genuine believer in Christ can say that. "Thou hast satisfied my mouth with good things; so that my youth is renewed as the eagle's." Believers in Jesus carry the pearl of content in their bosoms. Jesus takes away the restless spirit, and gives us rest. Jesus is the door that fits the heart, and when He is near to us He shuts out the world's cold and heat, and gives us sweet content. O ambitious man, you that runs after something, and you cannot tell what it is that can gratify your immortal spirit, turn to the cross, for at the foot of it there springs a sacred fount of soul-satisfying delight, and if you will but stoop and drink, your ambition shall be over, and you shall want no more. There is satisfaction for the deepest longings of heart, and head, and conscience, in the fount which springs from the wounds of Jesus. Faith is the silver cup. Dip it into the overflowing stream and drink. O Holy Spirit, put the cup to my poor thirsty brother's lip!

2. Secondly, water is also *life-preserving*. In the wilderness, where there is no water, the lips becomes chapped; the skin is dried; the tongue is like a firebrand and the mouth is like an oven; and the weary traveler must drink or die. O for a draught of water there! A bag of diamonds could not buy a flagon there! Priceless is the life-draught. And far out on the salt, salt sea, with

> Water, water everywhere,
> But not a drop to drink,

the mariner, though he may seek to satisfy himself with the brine around him, feels that it will be death sooner or later to him unless he can get some pure, clear, refreshing drops of water to drink. Drop you heavens in pity, or let some friendly bark espy the castaways. Such is the grace of God to the soul of man. The whole world over, there is nothing that can save a soul apart from the grace of God. Your good works can no more save you than the salt sea can give the sailor drink. Ceremonies can no more fill your heart with peace and give it life, than the hot sand of the wilderness can quench the thirst of the weary traveler. God must lead you to the river of eternal life flowing out of the Rock that was smitten. You must get grace through Jesus Christ, or hope shall never dawn upon you, but despair's midnight shall be your everlasting portion, where lost spirits wail out their undying lives in one endless death. O soul, if you get God's grace, you shall never die! Do you believe this? If that grace of God shall come flowing into your soul, you shall possess eternal life, an immortal principle which shall bid defiance to the grave, and make you sing in the very jaws of death, for he that drinks of this water, shall live in Christ forever. "He that liveth and believeth in me shall never die." "He that believeth in me, though he were dead, yet shall he live." This grace of God, then, is life-preserving, as well as thirst-quenching: Have you found it so? for, friend, I cannot afford to let you hear me, and yet escape a squeeze or two. If you forget this sermon, it shall not be because I did not press you to remember it.

3. Water, in the third place, *is filth-purging*. Man seeks no more than to get to the stream to wash when he is defiled. Many and many a time in passing through a country, the poor traveler comes to a brook so clear that he can see his face reflected in it, and he stoops down and laves his brow again and again, and takes his bath, and goes his way all bright and shining, as though he had exchanged sorrow for gladness, and received the oil of joy for mourning. Now, the guilty sinner, and such are we all by nature, however foul he may be, has but to stoop down at the river of eternal grace and wash, and he shall be clean. This stream can take out spots which nothing else can remove. Our sin is of such a crimson dye, naturally, that it might incarninate the Atlantic before it should be washed away, but this water of life can do it; it takes away the stain of blasphemy and lust; it removes the pollution of theft and murder. All manner of sin shall be forgiven unto that man who comes to the cross and trusts in Jesus. Whosoever believes in the world's great Redeemer, shall find full and complete pardon for every offense that he has committed. O try it, blackest of the black, if you be here! You who have gone to the greatest extent of sin, cast your guilty soul into this fountain, and see if you do not rise from it with your flesh like unto that of a little child, clean and pure, and not a spot remaining on you. This filth-removing is the grace of God streaming from the cross, where Jesus suffered in our stead the wrath which was due to us for our transgressions,

> Calvary's wonders let us trace,
> Justice magnified in grace;
> Mark the purple streams, and say,
> Thus my sins were washed away.

Friend, can you do this by faith, trusting for pardon to the blood of God's dear Son?

4. Water, again, is well known very frequently *to be softening*. There are some things which, when laid in water, soon lose their hardness, and are soft and pliable. This water of the grace of God, which it is my longing desire to commend to you, has a marvelous softening power. Adamant, millstone, ay, the nether millstone, northern iron and steel, have been melted when laid asoke in this fount. The hardest heart yields before the power of the love of God revealed in Christ Jesus. I think I hear one of you exclaim, "That is good news for me; I know that Christ can pardon me, but I cannot feel my sin as I ought: I am such a stiff-necked sinner, so hardened, so perverse, I cannot feel my need as I would wish to." Soul, if the grace of God shall flow upon your heart, it shall turn the stone, by a wondrous transformation, into flesh at once. There is no stubbornness which the grace of God cannot overcome. What a blessed thing it is for the preacher that he has not to give his hearers soft hearts, nor even to find tender hearts in them to begin with; how delightful it is for him to remember that he preaches a gospel which works wonders, wonders even greater than the rod of Moses; for when with the gospel we smite even a rock, penitential streams gush forth, and yet more, the rocky soul is itself dissolved under a sense of sin. O that some Saul of Tarsus might be washed by this stream now! He would no longer be the enemy of God's church, but would seek out some poor disciple to ask him what he must do to be saved. It is a heart-softening water. May the Lord give it to every one of us who have hard hearts remaining; fain would I bathe in it anew, that I might the more tenderly feel for you. Friend, will you never feel for yourself?

5. In the fifth place, this water has the property, like earthly water, *of being fire-quenching*. There is nothing like water after all, with all your new inventions, for putting out fire. We run for the engines, and turn on the main, what can we do better? But there are fires that burn within the human heart, deep volcanic fires fed from the depths of hell, furious flames which roar within the inner man, and anon roll over in torrents of sin-lava in his daily life—these are fires which never will be put out except by heavenly water. Oh, that fire of lust! How many a man has been consumed by it! It has devoured him as the fire devours the stubble. But when the grace of God comes, how soon that fire is damped, and even quenched forever! And there are other fires which burn in the soul—the fire of envy and of malice, the flames of anger and of unholy desire—how these will rage and glow until the grace of God comes! I know it puzzles many a man to know how he could live without such-and-such sins. "Oh," says he, "I could not live without them, I have fallen into the habit of them, and I must have them." Ah! but you shall be made a new man, such a new man, that if you were to meet your old self, you would avoid the wretch or struggle with him in deadly hand-to-hand encounter, out of sheer hatred to so mean a thing. Let me tell you, you will never be on good terms with your old self

so long as you live. You will hate that old self of yours, and it will be your daily desire to kill him. You will try to drive the nails through his hands and feet, and crucify him upon the cross of Jesus; and you will not be content unless you can kill him daily, mortifying him with his affections and his lusts. Oh, mighty grace of God that can put out the flames of sin! O sinner, the very flames of hell are put out by this grace of God; I mean so far as the saved soul is concerned: for the soul that is washed in this fountain, there is no hell in which God can punish it. How can He punish a pardoned sinner? How can he that is in Christ Jesus be cast into the flames?

No condemnation now I dread,
For justice smote my Surety's head.

"Who shall lay anything to the charge of God's elect?" He that has Christ to be his substitute is beyond all fear of hell. He can look down into that dread abyss, and feel that there is not a burning coal there for him, and that whoever may perish, yet he, being in Christ Jesus, can never die. Friend, have the fires in your soul met with this glorious antagonist? Are the engines of grace casting their floods upon your soul? Let conscience give its reply, and let it have your ear.

6. A sixth property is one that is not found in ordinary water, and that is, that it is a *spring-creating water*. Wherever the water of life falls, it makes a new spring, which begins to bubble up directly. By this I mean that if the grace of God enters into a man's heart, it is an immortal principle, and, as the Savior says, "Out of the midst of him shall flow rivers of living water." "The water that I shall give him shall be in him a well of water springing up into everlasting life." What a great difference there is between a pool and a running spring! Frequently in crossing the Alps, when one has been very faint and thirsty, it has been a sweet rest to sit down by a running spring, and wash one's face and feet, or bathe one's self in it. You may have walked until you are very footsore—you sit down to bathe your feet, and if you have found a mere pool, you will stir the bottom of it, and it will soon be very filthy; but when it is a running spring, you can sit and wash, and wash and wash again, and if you do stir the sand at the bottom, the earth is all gone in a moment, because the water still comes bubbling up fresh and fresh, and therefore it is always clean. So it is with the grace of God in a Christian: it never gets flat, and dull, and dead; and the daily pollutions, and washing of our feet, do not stain it, because it is a living spring, and arises from those "fresh springs" which David sings about which he rejoiced to find in the Lord his God. It is very hard work to play the part of a Christian if you have not a spring within you. For a man to have to keep up year after year a profession without life, why, it must be slavish work. Do you think that I would come and take a seat in this place, or in any other place of worship, and occupy it merely because it was respectable to do so, if I had no

care for it? I would as soon be a slave! Base is the man who even in his religion is the serf of tyrant fashion. To come up to the house of God because you love to be there, and to sing because you cannot help singing, and to unite with God's people because "birds of a feather" must "flock together," and you love to be among them—why there is something in that, something which tastes of reality and sincerity. He who has no great deeps of godliness in his soul makes a bondage of religion, he lives the life of a dog, and does not even get the crumbs from under the table as his portion. Mark you, brethren, it is harder to preach without this spring than it is to hear without it, because if you have not a spring in you, you may go foraging this dead man's books, and that other dead man's stores, to find a subject, but you will soon run dry; but if God the Holy Spirit is a spring within you, you may remain full of precious truth, and pour it out so long as God shall give you utterance, and you shall not run dry. What a blessing it is when the living water makes a spring within the Christian! What a curse to be one of the stagnant ponds of formality exhaling the putridity of hypocrisy. Friend, where are you, I must have my hand on you again, what are you in this matter as in the sight of God?

7. Seventhly, it is *fruit-producing water*. What fruit would there be upon the trees, what pasture in the meadows, what harvest in the field, if it were not for the rain? Everything would be barren without water, and even where there is fruit, if there be not also a fair share of water, what poor stuff it is! When I was in the country in June, and there were some heavy showers, I could not help thinking what good they were doing. There was the wheat just wanting plumping out, and the rain came to fill it, and to make the ears full. It might have been wheat of course without it, but the ear is likely to be more full of grain when the drought is gone. So, brethren, we may produce some little fruit when we have but little grace; but if we had more grace, how that fruit would plump out! How would our fruit be more rich, and fat, and mellow! How would our service to God be improved and perfected if we had more of this fruit-producing water! You cannot serve God without His grace. You cannot give Him true praise, nor true prayer, nor true service, nor anything that is acceptable, unless He first shall give you of the rain of His grace, grace for grace. "By their fruits shall ye know them:" friend, what fruit have you? O that grace may turn the barren fig tree into a good fruit-bearing tree!

8. And, lastly upon this point; *it is heaven-ascending water*. You know there is a rule of this sort in hydrostatics, that water will rise to its own level. Not long ago, I thought such things were gone out. I was riding along where the road was in a little cutting, and a spout was actually taken over the road to carry water from one field to the other. It was dripping fast upon the passengers, and making an ugly place in the road. Now, they might easily have taken the little stream under the road, and up again in a pipe; but,

I suppose, when the spout was made, it was not known to those who made it that water will rise as high as its source. Now, the grace of God will rise as high as its source. If you and I have grace that began with us, it will never get higher than we are. If you have grace that the priest gave you when you were christened, it will never get higher than the priest; but if you get the true grace of God which descends from heaven, it will take you as high as the New Jerusalem, from which it came. High up in the throne of God are the everlasting springs of divine mercy; at the foot of divine sovereignty it wells up a spring, clear as crystal, pure without a stain, and it flows down to earth, leaping down by the way of the cross. And it will ascend as high as its source. It will go up to the throne again, that is where it came from, and it will rise to its own level, and it will float you up there with it. If by the grace of God, you have been taken up by the stream of Jesus' dying love, it will take you up to its own source, and where God is, there you shall be. Because you have been made to taste, to feel, and to be saturated with the grace that came from God, from a divine source, you shall also have a divine portion forever. The rivers go to the sea because they originally came from the sea. Did not the sun kiss the sea, and make it ascend to him in clouds that it might descend in rain? And so, all the rivers of grace in us shall flow into the sea, whence they came, the bottomless, shoreless sea of everlasting love, because that is the eternal source and fountain of them all. Clouds of suffering went up from the heart of Jesus to return to earth in showers of mercy for poor sinners. Friend, do you know anything about this in your very soul?

Now, I have thus spoken of the grace of God which is revealed in Jesus Christ. I only hope that someone here may say, "I wish I were washed in it! I wish my thirst were satisfied with it I wish that my soul were made to overflow with it! I wish that I might be lifted up to heaven though its energy!" Oh! then, soul, I am glad you have the desire. Turn it into a prayer, and let the prayer be the text, "Give me this water!"

Your Likelihood of Obtaining This Water

And now, with great brevity indeed, we shall take the second point, that is, TO CHEER YOUR HEARTS WITH SOME REFLECTIONS UPON THE LIKELIHOOD OF YOUR GETTING THIS LIVING WATER.

I am supposing now that you really want it. If you say, "Sir, give me this water," you will have it; and I will tell you why I think you will have it—because, in the first place, *I do not think that an ordinary man would deny another water.* If I stood by a well, and you approached me, and said, "Sir, give me this water," I should say, "As much as you like of it." Who would not give water? It is the very commonest of gifts. Even in the East, with all the value that is attached to water there, the Savior mentions that as one of the most ordinary acts of benevolence. "Whosoever shall give to drink unto one of these little ones a cup of cold water only in the name of a disciple, verily I say unto you, He shall in no wise lose his reward." Who will deny another a glass of water? Then note, that according to our text, the giving of saving grace is to the great Redeemer no more than the giving of water to you! Grace is a priceless boon for you to receive, but to Jesus it is a delight to give it. If you give water, you have a little less water left, but if Christ gives grace, He has not any grace the less. He still has as much grace in the inexhaustible fullness which dwells in His adorable person. As the sun is just as bright for all its shining, and the ocean still full notwithstanding all the clouds exhaled from it, so Jesus is as abundant as ever in pardoning mercy and saving power. I tell you that for Jesus Christ to be gracious, is as much according to His nature as it is for you and for me to be generous enough to give away water. The blessing of poor needy souls is no labor with Jesus, no loss to Him, no tax upon Him; all the pain and cost He has borne long ago, and now to save the guilty is His reward in which He sees the recompense of His travail. Now, if in this place the grace of God had been compared to gold, that metaphor would have suited well to express its value; but you would have said, "Who gives gold away?" But here it is compared with water, water which man freely gives, and which our Lord Jesus never denies to those who seek it of Him. I do not believe, then, if an ordinary man will give away water—and Christ compares His grace with water, that He will let you say, "Sir, give me this water!" and then send you away without it. Friend, be not so unbelieving as to think that the Lord Jesus is ungenerous and unkind, but ask for the living water, and it shall be given you.

Again, *if you would refuse water to some persons, I am very sure that you would not refuse it to a thirsty person.* If you saw him panting, and the hot sweat starting to his brow, and if he could scarcely speak, but had only strength enough to gasp out, "Sir, if you would but give me a cup of water, I would bless you for it with all my heart," why, you would run and bring out the sparkling crystal, and feel a great pleasure in seeing him drink. Would you not? I am sure you would. Now, if you are a thirsty soul, I am quite sure Christ will give you the water of life. He will give it to any that ask, for He refuses none; but to you He will give it so quickly, that He will seem to give it twice over. He will not let you thirst in vain, for has He not promised, "When the poor and needy seek water, and there is none, and their tongue faileth for thirst, I the Lord will hear them, I the God of Israel will not forsake them. I will open rivers in high places, and fountains in the midst of the valleys: I will make the wilderness a pool of water, and the dry land springs of water?' "Oh," says one, "how I desire to be saved! How I long to have Christ!" You may have Him then, for Jesus Christ never did deny a thirsty sinner, never did refuse to give of His substance to the poor, His clothes to the naked, or His medicine to the sick. He came on purpose to bless such. I say, there are all likelihoods that you shall have the blessing if you will but pray earnestly, "Lord, give me this water"; nay, more, there is a certainty of it.

Another reason gives me comfort for you, and that is—*there certainly is a plenty of it*, for the apostle John says he saw "a *river* of the water of life." Now, nobody is afraid, when there is a deep, broad, flowing river to draw from. Who fears to exhaust the Thames or drain the Danube by his thirst? Moreover, as John Bunyan reminds us, a river is free to everybody to drink. The source of it is private. Many rivers rise in a park or private grounds, but the river itself is public. As soon as it becomes a considerable stream, it becomes a public highway, and a universal water supply. It is free, it flows the way it wills. Rivers possess a sort of sovereignty, you cannot bid them flow in a straight line, or order them by rules of geometry; they will have their own sweet will. If the river chooses to go by one town and not by another, it will have its way, try to stop it who may? But while it is sovereign in its course and direction, yet it is free for public use; the cattle come to drink, and even a poor dog is not refused when he gets to the river's brink; if he wants to lap and cool his feverish tongue in the dog days, who shall say him nay? And you, poor sinner, you shall find the grace of God free to you, for there is enough of it; It is up to the banks; nay, it overflows the banks; there is a flood of it, such a flood that there never can by any possibility be any lack, though all men should come. Though ten thousand times ten thousand should come, there would still be found sufficient grace in Jesus to meet the case of all, for whom the Lord brings, the Lord can provide for in Christ Jesus. The grace of God is sovereign in its choice, and discriminating in its course, but still it is free to all thirsty ones who long to partake of its everlasting fullness.

I am comforted, also, by another thought, namely, *that this river flows on purpose* for the thirsty. I am sure I do not know what there is mercy in the world for, unless it is for those who want it because of their sin and misery. What could Christ have made an atonement for, except for sinners? It is not possible that the beloved Physician came all the way from heaven to heal those who were well and needed no medicine. It is not likely that He opens His great granaries to feed the nations who have a harvest of their own; it must be that our Joseph has stored up the wheat for hungry perishing ones. O you that need, come and welcome, for the fountain is opened especially for you: it flows, that such as you may come and drink. Friend, shall our invitations have no power with you? O Holy Spirit, make men willing in this the day of your power!

I feel sure, too, that you who seek the Lord, will find His grace, *because there never has been one refused yet*. A dear brother, who, I believe, is now present, told me that he owed his conversion in early life to hearing a sentence or two of a sermon from a man whose name he never knew, but whom he heard preach standing on a log of wood on a village green. He had never gone to listen to the gospel anywhere, but happened to be straying through the village, and he heard the man say that there never was a soul that sincerely sought God through Jesus Christ, but what ultimately, sooner or later, it was brought into a state of peace. And let me say to you all—it may sink into some heart, and one day yield it comfort—it shall not be said by you in eternity, that you sought the Lord and He would not hear you. I recollect what comfort this gave to me when I heard my mother say that she had heard many wicked things in the world, but she never heard a man wicked enough to say that he had sincerely sought God through Jesus Christ, and yet had been refused. When I heard that, I thought I would say it, for I was confident that I had sought the Lord, but I had had no comfortable answer. But I have never said it, I have never had cause to say it, for before I could be driven to that state of despair, I looked unto Him and was lightened, and so I am persuaded it is shall be with you. There never was one refused who said, "Give me this water," and you shall not be the first.

To close this point, *it is to Jesus Christ's glory to give of His saving mercy, and therefore be certain that He will not withhold it.* It cannot make Christ more glorious to deny a poor sinner His mercy. It cannot be to His profit to shut His door in a seeking sinner's face. It is impossible that the bleeding Lamb should cease to be pitiful to poor bleeding hearts. By everything that can make the name of the great Physician glorious, by every pang of His soul on account of sinners, I am persuaded that He will not deny you. Why, the more a physician cures, the greater is his fame; the more the Savior saves, the higher is His honor; the more Jesus Christ can bless, the more lofty will be the praise, and the more exalted that mighty shout of "Hallelujah!" that shall go up from ten thousand times ten thousand of sinners, who have been washed in His blood. Come, then, seeking sinner, come now, and by humble faith trust in the Mediator's sacrifice. Wipe those eyes of yours. Be of good cheer. Be bold in heart. He calls you. There is room at His table. The door is open. There is room in His heart. He died for those who rest in Him. If you wish for Christ, He wishes for you. If you long to go to the feast, He wants guests as much as you want the feast. Only trust Him! God help you to trust Him by His Spirit, and you shall live.

Lord, Give Me This Water

The last thing was to be this: to urge you tonight, before you leave this house—but my urging will be of no service unless God the Holy Spirit own it—TO URGE YOU TO PRAY THE PRAYER OF THE TEXT.

A desire is like seed in the bag, but prayer sows it in the furrow. A desire is like water in the bottle, but prayer drinks thereof. Now, I commend to you the prayer of my text—"Sir, give me this water." Begin, then, your prayer *by honoring Christ.* Do not call Him "Sir," but call Him "Lord." She gave

Him the highest title that her respect could accord. She did not know Him in any other capacity, but she called Him "Sir." Now, call Jesus "Lord," for you will get no mercy if you dishonor Christ. Think of Him as God's only Son suffering for sinners. Call Him "Lord." Can you do that? If you reject His divinity, you shut yourself out of His kingdom. He must be owned as Lord and God as well as Savior. "Oh!" you say, "I have long ago called Him Lord, I know Him to be divine; I rejoice in the thought of His eternal power and Godhead; I would honor Him with all that I have." Well, then, you have well begun, but may grace make you go further.

Now, in the next place, if you would pray this prayer aright, notice it, and *confess thine undeservingness*. It is not, "Sir, sell me this water," but, "Sir, *give* me this water." Confess that it is a gift. You shall never have it otherwise. Away with your merit-mongering. Away with your trusting in your prayers, and your tears, and your sense of need. Mercy must be given, or else you shall never have it. "Sir, *give* me, *give* me, *give* me this water. O Lord, give me grace, or else I die; give it me of Your free mercy, because You have promised to save the chief of sinners; give it me, Lord. I have done with boasting; I have done with the Pharisee's thanking You that I am not as other men are; I come empty-handed; I come naked, poor, miserable; give it me; I have nothing to buy it with. Oh! give me, without money and without price, Your salvation." Friend, does your pride kick at this? Be wise, I pray you, and bow your neck to the yoke of grace.

Take care, too, that you make it *a personal prayer*—"Lord, give it *me*." Never mind your neighbors just now. Care for them when you are saved. Look after their salvation when your own is secure; but just now you have first to do with yourself. Your children? Ay, pray for them. Your relatives? Yes, consider them, But, meanwhile, now it is *yourself*, your own proper self that is concerned. Do not think of the whole congregation. Think now personally of your own soul, and say, "Lord, give *me* this water." I mean you, Mary, and you, Thomas, and you, John, let the prayer come from your own lips, as distinctly being from yourself. As you sit or stand now in this house, silently breathe the petition—"Lord, give Your grace to *me, even me*."

> Pass me not, O gracious Father,
>   Sinful though my heart may be;
> Thou might'st curse me, but the rather
>   Let thy mercy light on me,
>   Even me.
>
> Pass me not, O tender Savior!
>   Let me love and cling to thee;
> I am longing for thy favor;
>   When thou comest, call for me,
>   Even me.

Once more, I want you to offer this prayer *in the present tense*—not "Give me this water tomorrow"; but "Tonight give it me; Lord, save my soul now." The worst of most of men is this: they would be saved, but it must be when they die. You would serve the devil all your life, and then cheat him of your soul at the last! Mean, miserable thought! If God be God, serve Him, serve Him now; and may the Lord have us in life, as we hope He may have us in our death. "Give me this water." But you are going out next Wednesday; that will be awkward! "Yes," said some young woman at a revival meeting, who was in much concern, "but I am going to a ball tomorrow"; and so everything good was put off for that; but she dropped down dead at the ball! God grant there may be no such cases of postponing here, lest we postpone ourselves into eternity, where there are no acts of pardon past. May we have Christ *now*. We may not live to see tomorrow's sun. Albeit that the sun is well-nigh gone down, yet the light of this evening may not have gone before our life may be ended. How near to death we stand, and yet we scarcely think of it! Right on the edge of our graves sometimes we are, and yet we sport and laugh as though we had a lease of life! You forget death, most of you. The cemetery is so far out of town, but still you should not quite forget, for the hearse goes to and fro with awful regularity, and the church bell that tolls is not rusty, and those words, "Earth to earth, dust to dust, ashes to ashes," are still familiar to the ears of some of us. It will soon be your turn to die. You, too, must gather up your feet in the bed, and meet your father's God; God grant that you may then be found right with Him, Little do I know for whom these sentences may have a special bearing, but they may have a bearing, dear friend, upon you. I see some of you dressed in black; you have had to go to the grave mourning because of others: that black will be worn by others soon for you, and the place that now knows you shall know you no more forever. Oh! by the frailty of life, by the near approach of the Master, or by the certainty of death, I pray you see to it that you breathe the prayer, "Lord give me of thy grace." The Lord help you to pray it. Amen.

4

*A Woman's Memorial**

Verily I say unto you, Wheresoever this gospel shall be preached in the whole world, there shall also this, that this woman hath done, be told her a memorial of her (Matthew 26:13).

The evangelists are of course the historians of the time of Christ; but what strange historians they are! They leave out just that which worldly ones would write, and they record just that which the worldly would have passed over. What historian would have thought of recording the story of the widow and her two mites? Would a Hume or a Smollett have spared half a page for such an incident? Or think you that even a Macaulay could have found it in his pen to write down a story of an eccentric woman, who broke an alabaster box of precious ointment upon the head of Jesus? But so is it. Jesus values things, not by their glare and glitter, but by their intrinsic value. He bids His historians store up, not the things which shall dazzle men, but those which shall instruct and teach them in His spirit. Christ values a matter, not by its exterior, but by the motive which dictated it, by the love which shines from it. O singular historians! you have passed by much that Herod did; you tell us little of the glories of His temple; you tell us little of Pilate, and that little not to his credit; you treat with neglect the battles that are passing over the face of the earth; the grandeur of Caesar does not entice you from your simple story. But you continue to tell these little things, and wise are you in so doing, for verily these little things, when put into the scales of wisdom, weigh more than those monstrous bubbles of which the world delights to read.

And now my prayer is that we may be endued this morning with the same spirit as that which prompted the woman, when she broke her alabaster box upon the head of Christ. There must be something wonderful about this story, or else Christ would not have linked it with His gospel; for

---

* This sermon was taken from *The New Park Street Pulpit* and was preached on Sunday morning, November 27, 1859.

so has He done. So long as this gospel lives shall this story of the woman be told; and when this story of the woman ceases to exist, then the gospel must cease to exist also, for they are co-eternal. As long as this gospel is preached, and wherever it is proclaimed, the story of this woman is to go with it. Our Lord's prediction goes on to be verified, while the memorial of this woman fills the church with its fragrance. There must be something, therefore, remarkable in it: let us pause, and look, and learn, and God give us grace to imitate.

I shall want you first attentively to *observe the woman*; secondly, I shall invite you to *look into the face of her loving Lord, and to listen to what he says about her*; and then I shall close with an earnest suggestion that *each one of us look to himself*, for surely this is meant for our profit, and is not of any private interpretation.

Observe the Woman Herself

First, then, my friends, LET US OBSERVE THE WOMAN HERSELF.

There is much dispute among commentators as to who she was. Some there are who confound this woman with that other woman who was a sinner, who came behind Christ, and washed His feet with tears, and wiped them with the hairs of her head. There are some too, who think that the woman in Matthew is the same as the one of whom I read just now in the gospel of John; while there are others who say, "Not so, for that incident occurred in the house of Lazarus, where Lazarus sat at the table, and Martha served, while this, on the other hand, is stated to have taken place in the house of Simon the leper that was at Bethany." You will recollect also that this narrative in Matthew happened two days before the Passover (*see* the second verse of this twenty-sixth chapter) while the transaction recorded by the evangelist John, is said to have taken place six days before the Passover. It will be an interesting study for you some Lord's day afternoon, if you are at home, to sit down and find out these different women, and see how far they are all alike, or wherein there is a difference. I have no time to spare on that subject this morning, and if I had I should not use it, for it will do you good to search the Scriptures and find it out for yourselves. Whether this, however, was Mary the sister of Martha or not. I will leave undetermined. We shall not err in speaking of her as a certain woman. Christ was sitting, or reclining, at the table of Simon the leper. A sudden thought strikes this woman. She goes to her home; she gets her money, and expends it in an alabaster box of ointment, or perhaps she had it in store, all ready laid up. She brings it; she hastens into the house. Without asking anyone's leave, or communicating her intention, she breaks the alabaster vase, which was itself of great value, and forth flows a stream of the most precious ointment, with a very refreshing fragrance. This she poured on His head. So plenteous was the effusion that it streamed right down to His feet, and the whole house was filled with the odor of the ointment. The disciples murmured, but the Savior commended. Now, what was there in the action of this woman worthy of commendation, and of such high commendation too that her memory must be preserved and transmitted with the gospel itself throughout all ages?

I think, in the first place, this act was done from the impulse of a loving heart, and this it was that made it so remarkable. Ah! my brethren, the heart is better than the head, after all, and the renewed heart is infinitely superior to the head; for, somehow or other, though doubtless grace will renew the understanding, yet it takes longer to sanctify the understanding, than it does the affections; or, at least, the heart is the first affected; it is that which is first touched, and being swifter in its goings forth than the head; it is generally more uncontaminated by the atmosphere around, and more clearly perceives that which is right. We in our day fall into the habit of calculating whether a thing is our duty or not; but have we never an impulse of the heart more impressive, and more expressive, than the mere arithmetic of moral obligations? Our heart says to us, "Arise, go and visit such and such an one who is sick:" we stop and say, "Is it my duty? If I do not go, will not somebody else go? Is the service absolutely requisite?" Or your heart has said perhaps, once upon a time, "Devote of thy substance largely to the cause of Christ." If we obeyed the heart we should do it at once; but instead of that, we stop and shake the head, and we begin to calculate the question whether it is precisely our duty. *This woman* did no such thing. It was not her duty—I speak broadly—it was not her positive duty to take the alabaster box and break it on the head of Christ. She did not do it from a sense of obedience; she did it from a loftier motive. There was an impulse in her heart, which gushed forth like a pure stream overflowing every quibble and questioning—"Duty or no duty, go and do it"—and she takes the most precious things she can find, and out of simple love, guided by her renewed heart, she goes at once and breaks the alabaster box, and pours the ointment on His head. If she had stayed a minute to consider, she never would not have done it at all; if she had pondered, and reckoned, and reasoned, she never would have accomplished it; but this was the heart acting, the invincible heart, the force of a spontaneous impulse, if not of a very inspiration, while the head with its various organs has not been allowed time to hold a council. It was the heart's dictate fully and entirely carried out. Now, in these times, we lace ourselves so tight that we do not give our hearts room to act; we just calculate whether we *should* do it—whether it is precisely our duty. Oh! would to God our hearts could grow bigger! Let our heads be as they are, or let them be improved; but let the heart have full play, and how much more would be done for Christ than ever has been done as yet! But I would have you remark, that this woman, acting from her heart, did not act as a matter of form.

You and I generally look to see whether the thing our new heart tells us to do has ever been done before; and then, if, like Martha, we love Christ, we still think it will be the proper mode of showing our love to prepare Him a supper, and go and stand and wait at the table. We look for a precedent. We recollect that the Pharisee gave Christ a supper; we remember how many others of the disciples have given Him a dinner; and then we think that is the proper orthodox way, and we will go and do the same. "Mr. So-and-So gives ten guineas; *I* shall give ten guineas. Mrs. So-and-So teaches in Sunday school; *I* shall teach in the Sunday school. Mr. This or That is in the habit of having prayer with his servants; *I* shall do likewise." You see, we look to find out whether anybody else has set us an example, and then we get into the habit of doing all these things as a matter of form. But Mary never thought of that; she never asked whether there was anybody else that had ever broken an alabaster box of ointment on that sacred head. No, she goes her way; her heart says, "Do it," and she does it all alone, breaks the box, and out flows the precious ointment. I would that we also obeyed the dictates of the heart; but no, we take second thoughts. Depend on it, in the things of Christ first thoughts are the best. It is that heavenly inspiration of the Spirit which comes into the soul, and says, "Do some great things for your Master—go out and show your love to Him in some hazardous expedition." Oh! if we did but obey that, what results should we not see? We sit down and say, "Is it reasonable? Is it expected of me? Is it my duty?" No, my friend, it is *not* expected of you; it is *not* your duty; but are you going to stop short in bare duty? Will you give to Christ no more than His due, as you give to Caesar when you pay your tax? What! if the *custom* be but a shekel, is the shekel all He is to have? Is such a Master as this to be served by calculations? Is He to have His everyday penny, just as the common laborer? God forbid we should indulge such a spirit! Alas! for the mass of Christians, they do not even rise so high as that; and if they once get there they fold their arms, and they are quite content. "I do as much as anybody else, in fact a little more; I am sure I do my duty; nobody can find any fault; if people were to expect me to do more, they would be really unreasonable." Ah! then, you have not yet learned this woman's love, in all its heights and depths. You know not how to do an unreasonable thing—a thing that is not expected of you—out of the divine impulse of a heart fully consecrated to Jesus. The first era of the Christian church was an era of wonders, because then, Christian men obeyed the prompting of their hearts. What wonders they used to do! A voice within the heart said to an apostle, "Go to a heathen country and preach." He never counted the cost—whether his life would be safe, or whether he would be successful; he went and did whatever his heart told him. To another it spoke, "Go, and distribute all that you have"; and the Christian went and did it, and cast his all into the common store. He never asked whether it was his duty; his heart bid him do it, and he obeyed at once. Now, we have become stereotyped; we run in the ancient cart-rut; we all do what other people do; we are just content with performing the routine, and accomplishing the formalism of religious duties. How unlike this woman, who went out of all order, because her heart told her to do so, and she obeyed from her heart. This, I think, is the first part of the woman's act that won a deserved commendation.

The second commendation is—what this woman did was done purely to Christ, and for Christ. Why did she not take this spikenard, and sell it, and give the money to the poor? "No," she might have thought, "I love the poor, I would relive them at any time; to the utmost of my ability would I clothe the naked, and feed the hungry; but I want to do something for *Him*." Well, why did she not get up, and take the place that Martha did, and begin to wait at the table? Ah! she thought, Martha was at the table, dividing her services; Simon the leper, and Lazarus, and all the rest of the guests, have a share in her attention. I want to do something directly *for Him*, something that He will have all to Himself, something that He cannot give away, but which He must have and which must belong to Him. Now, I do not think that any other disciple, in all Christ's experience, ever had that thought. I do not find, in all the Evangelists, another instance like this. He had disciples, whom He sent out by two and two to preach, and right valiantly did they do it, for they desired to benefit their fellowmen in the service of their Lord. He had disciples too, I doubt not, who were very, very happy, when they distributed the bread and the fishes to the hungry multitudes, because they felt they were doing an act of humanity, in supplying the needs of the hungry; but I do not think He had one disciple that thought about doing something exactly and directly for *Him*—something, of which no one else could partake, something that should be Christ's, and Christ's alone. This is something, my brethren, which I wish you to remember. How much of what we do in the cause of religion, fails to have any excellence in it, because we do not perform it for Christ's sake! We go up to preach, perhaps, and we do not feel that we are preaching for Christ. Perhaps we are preaching with a sincere desire to do good to our fellow men: so far so good: but even that is not so grand a motive, as the desire to do it for Him who loved us, and gave Himself for us. Do you not often catch yourself, when you put a coin into the hand of the poor, thinking there is a virtue in it? And so there is, in one sense; but do you not find yourself forgetting, that you should do that for *Him*, and give that as unto Christ, giving unto the poor, and lending unto the Lord? Sunday school teachers! I ask you also: do you not find, in teaching your class that you often forget that you should be teaching for *Him*? Your act is done rather for the church, for the school, for your fellow men, for the poor, for the children's sake, than for Christ's sake. But the very beauty of this woman's act lay in this, that she did it all for the Lord Jesus Christ. You could not say she did it for Lazarus, or did it for the disciples; no, it was exclusively for *Him.* She felt she owed Him all; it was He who had forgiven her sins; it was He who had opened her eyes, and given her to see the light of heavenly day; it was He who was her hope, her joy, her all; her love went out in its common actings to her fellow men—it went out toward the poor, the sick, and the needy; but oh! it went in all its vehemence to Him. That Man, that blessed Man, the God-man, she *must* give something to *Him.* She could not be content to put it in that bag there; she must go and put it right on *His* head. She could not be content that Peter, or James, or John, should have a part of it; the whole pound must go on *His* head: and though others might say it was waste, yet she felt it was not, but that whatever she could give unto Him was well bestowed, because it went to Him to whom she owed her all! Ah! my dear hearers, learn this lesson, I pray you. The scene is a very simple one, but it is extremely captivating. You will do your acts in religion far better, if you can cultivate always the desire to do them all for Christ. Oh! to preach for Christ! What precious work that is! When the mind is fatigued and the body weary, this will make a man strong to labor and to suffer too, if he hears the whisper, "Go and do it for your Master's sake." Oh! to visit the sick for Christ, and distribute to the poor for His sake! This will make toil light; self-denial will become a pleasure; it will cease to be self-denial altogether, if we remember that we are doing it for Him! But we do not now as this woman did; I fear our love is but faint and cold. If the spark were kindled to a flame, we should never be content with attending to religion from a selfish motive; we should not assay to do holy works with the idea of getting good ourselves; but our one aim and desire would be, to glorify Him—to spend and be spent for Him who suffered on the cross for us. These two commendations were surely enough to immortalize this woman—she obeyed the dictates of her heart, and she did it all to *Him.*

There is yet a third thing. I have anticipated myself. This woman did an extraordinary thing for Christ. Not content with doing what other people had done, nor wishful to find a precedent, she ventured to expose her ardent attachment though she might have known that some would call her mad, and all would think her foolish and wasteful, yet she did it—an extraordinary thing—for the love she bear her Lord. Our church acts at this day—as far as I know the church of Christ, from extensive traveling and considerable experience, exhibit a dull, uniform, dead level. There are some few men who strike out every now and then a new course, who are not content to ask what the fathers did, what is canonical, what will be permitted and allowed by ecclesiastical polity or by public opinion—men will only ask, "Does my heart bid me do it for Christ, then I will go and do it?" and it is done. But the mass of Christians have not got a new thought, simply because new thoughts generally come from the heart, and they will not let their hearts work, and consequently they never get a new emotion. I believe that the origin of Sunday schools is to be found in the heart of some one man. His heart prompted him, saying, "Take these little ragged urchins, and teach them the Word of God." If that thought had come into some of you, you would have said, "Well, there is not any Sunday school connected with the church of Christ all over England; I am sure the minister will throw many obstacles in the way; nobody else has done it, but it would have been a good thing if it had been done many years ago." Robert Raikes never talked like that; he went and did it; and we, poor little creatures, can imitate him afterward. If we would let our heart work, we should do new things. Within fifty years from this date, unless the Lord come before the era, there will be new operations for the cause of Christ, of which, if we heard them now, we should jump for joy. Perhaps they will never come to pass for years, simply because this is the age for intellectual reasoning, and not the Spirit within, there might be fifty schemes for the promotion of the cause of Christ started in as many days, and all those fifty, through the Holy Spirit's blessing, might be useful to the souls of men.

"But," says one, "you would make us all fanatics." Yes, no doubt that is just the name you would very soon earn, and a very respectable name too, for it is a name that has been borne by all men who have been singularly good. All those who have done wonders for Christ have always been called eccentric and fanatical. Why, when Whitfield first went on Kennington Common to preach, because he could not find a building large enough, it was quite an unheard of thing, to preach in the open air. How could you expect God to hear prayer, if there was not a roof over the top of the people's heads? How could souls be blessed, if the people had not seats, and regular high-backed pews to sit in! Whitfield was thought to be doing something outrageous, but he went and did it; he went and broke the alabaster box on the head of his Master, and in the midst of scoffs and jeers, he preached in the open air. And what came of it? A revival of godliness, and a mighty spread of religion. I wish we were all of us ready to do some extraordinary thing for Christ—willing to be laughed at, to be called fanatics, to be hooted and scandalized because we went out of the common way, and were not content with doing what everybody else could do or approve to be done.

And here let me remark, that Jesus Christ certainly deserves to be served after an extraordinary manner. Was there ever a people that had such a leader or such a lover as we have in the person of Christ? And yet, my dear friends, there have been many impostors in the world, who have had disciples more ardently attached to them than some of you are to Christ Jesus. When I read the life of Mohammed, I see men who loved him so, that they would expose their persons to death at any moment for the false prophet, dash into battle almost naked, cut their way through hosts of enemies, and do exploits out of a passionate zeal for him whom they verily believed to be sent of God. And even that modern delusion of Joe Smith lacks not its martyrs. When I read the history of the Mormonite emigrants, and of all the miseries they endured when driven out of the city of Nauvoo; how they had to pass over trackless snows and pathless mountains, and were ready to die under the guns of the United States marauders, and how they suffered for that false prophet, I do stand ashamed of the followers of Christ, that they should permit the followers of an impostor to suffer hardships, and loss of limb and life, and everything else that men count dear, for an impostor, while they themselves show that they do not love their Master, their true and loving Lord half so well, else would they serve Him in an extraordinary manner, as He deserves. When the soldiers of Napoleon performed such unexampled deeds of daring in his day, people ceased to wonder. They said, "No wonder that they do that; see what their leader does." When Napoleon, sword in hand, crossed over the bridge of Lodi, and bid them follow, no one wondered that every common soldier was a hero. But it is wonderful, when we consider what the Captain of our salvation has done for us, that we are content to be such every day nothings as the most of us are. Ah! if we did but think of His glory, and of what He deserves—if we did but think of His sufferings, and of what He merits at our hands, surely we should do something out of the common; we should break our alabaster box, and pour the pound of ointment on His head again.

But not only does an extraordinary thing cease to appear extraordinary, when you think of the person to whom it is done, but surely when you think of the person who is bound to do it, an extraordinary thing becomes very ordinary indeed. My friends, if I should leave this place, and go into the midst of the abode of some wild Red Indians, and there be exposed to cold and hunger, and famine, and nakedness; if through long years I should preach the gospel to a people who rejected me, and if afterward I should be raised alive at the stake by them, I do acknowledge and confess that I feel it were but a slight thing I should have done for Him to whom I owe so much. When I think of what my Master has done for me, surely the stripes and imprisonments, the perils, the shipwrecks, the journeyings, which even a Paul suffered, seem to be less than nothing and vanity compared with the debt of love I owe. Now, I do not expect all of you to love Christ as I think I ought, for perhaps you do not owe Him so much as I do; perhaps you have never been such great sinners as I was, perhaps you have never had so much forgiven, and have never tasted so much of His love, and have never had so much fellowship with Him; but this I know—if every atom of my body could become a man, and every man so made could suffer and be cut piece meal, all that suffering would not be a worthy recompense for what He has done for me. I think there are some of you that might stand up and tell the like tale. I can look round on some of you that were drunkards, that were swearers, but you have obtained mercy;

and, my dear friends, if you do something extraordinary for Christ, while other people wonder with a vacant stare of astonishment, you may say, "Do you wonder at me?"

> Love I much? I've more forgiven;
> I'm a miracle of grace.

You for whom Jesus has done little, if any such there be, love Him little; but I do beseech you—those of you whom *He* has loved with an extraordinary affection, and who feel that you owe much to His grace, that He has done great things for you, whereof you are glad, do not be content with doing what other people do. Think of others thus. "I have no doubt that what they do is their best; but I must do more than they, for I owe Him more than they do." And oh! if everyone of us could feel this, we should account labor light and pain easy, and be disgusted with ourselves that we spend so much of our lives doing nothing for Him who has bought us with His most precious blood.

I have but one more reason to add. It seems to me that Jesus praised this woman, and handed down this memorial, because her act was so beautifully expressive. There was more virtue in it than you could see. The manner, as well as the matter, of her votive sacrifice, might well excite the rebuke of men, whose practical religion is mercenary and economical. It is not enough that she pours out the ointment with such reckless profusion, but she is so rash and extravagant she must needs break the box. Marvel not, beloved, but admire the rapt enthusiasm of her godly soul. Why! love is a passion. If you did but know and feel its vehemence, you would never marvel at an act so expressive. Her love could no more tarry to conform to the rubrics of service, than it could count the cost of her offering. A mighty impulse of devotion carries her soul far above all ordinary routine. Her conduct did but symbol the inspiration of a grateful homage. A sanctified heart, more beautiful than the transparent vase of alabaster, was that hour broken. Only from a broken heart can the sweet spices of grace give forth their rich perfume. "Love and grief, our heart dividing," we sometimes sing—but oh! let me say it—love, grief and gratitude, the spikenard, myrrh, and frankincense of the gospel blend together here; the heart must expand and break, or the colors would never fill the house. Every muscle of her face, every involuntary motion of her frame, frenzied as it might appear to the unsympathizing looker-on, was in harmony with her heart's emotion. Her every feature gives evidence of her sincerity. What they could coldly criticize, Jesus delivers them for a study. Here is one whom a Savior's love has produced its appropriate effects. Here is a heart that has brought forth the most precious fruits. Not only admiration for her, but kindness to us, moved our Lord, when He resolved henceforth to illustrate the gospel, wherever it is published, with this portrait of saintly love, in one instant breaking the delicate vase, and bursting the tender heart. Why, that woman meant to say to Christ, "Dear Lord, I give myself away." She went home; she brought out the most precious thing she had; if she had had anything worth ten thousand times as much she would have brought that; in fact, she did really bring Him all.

Look into the Face of Her Loving Lord

Having described this woman as so well worthy to be remembered forever, I NOW INVITE YOU TO LOOK INTO THE FACE OF HER LOVING LORD. Hark! what is all that muttering about? What are they saying to one another over yonder? Why, there is Judas, he has been taking out a little scrap of paper, and casting up a sum, and he makes out that that box of ointment is worth just three hundred pence. And what are Peter, and Thomas, and the other disciples talking about? "Oh dear," they say, "see what a waste; I am very sorry; if I had known what she was going to do I would have taken that box away from her, indeed I would; I would not have allowed that; what a waste! and all for this little smell—it is soon gone, and a little of it would have done. What multitudes of hungry mouths might have been filled, if it had been sold and give to the poor." "Oh!" says one of them, "I never saw such an insane thing in my life. I wonder the Lord Jesus was not angry with her." Do you hear that talk? Do you hear it? I have heard it many times before, and I hear it now. It is a kind of talk that is sometimes very rife in the church of Christ. If there is a man that does a little more than anyone else, people say, "There is no occasion for it at all; there is no need for it." If someone gives more than anyone else to the cause of Christ, they say, "Ah! I cannot understand such a motive as would lead him to do that; there is a medium in all things; there is a limit to which people should go, and they ought not to exceed it." And so they begin chatting and talking one with another, and if there is anything done that seems extraordinary, they will begin to pick a hole in it. Instead of emulating superior devotion themselves, they begin to murmur, and to consider how much might have been done with the same effort, if it had been conducted in an orthodox manner. That young man, instead of preaching at the corner of the street, if he taught in a Sunday school, how much good might he do? If—instead of rambling all over the country, some would have said, "If Whitfield had kept to his own congregation, or to his own parish, he might have done a great deal of good." Yes, I dare say; but you and Judas talk that matter over together; we have no time to trouble ourselves with it this morning; let us look at what Jesus Christ Himself says. He says, "Trouble her not, trouble her not. I have three very good excuses for her; only listen to them." And the three interpretations our Lord gave of the woman were these.

"She has wrought a good work upon me." Note these two last words "*Upon me!*" "Why," say they, "it is not a good work to go and spill all that ointment, and perpetrate so much waste." "No," says Jesus, "it is not a good work in relation to you, but it is a good work upon me." And, after all, that is the best sort of good work—a good work that is wrought upon Christ—an act of homage such as faith in His name, and love to His person, would dictate. A good work upon the poor is commendable; a good work upon the church is excellent; but a good work upon Christ, surely this is one of the very highest and noblest kinds of good works. But I will be bound to say that neither Judas nor the disciples could comprehend this; and there is a mystic virtue in the acts of some Christian men that common Christians do not and cannot comprehend. That mystic virtue consists in this, that they do it "as unto the Lord, and not unto men," and in their services they serve the Lord Jesus Christ.

Moreover, our Lord protects the woman with another apology. "Do not trouble her; do not reflect upon what might have been done for the poor, 'for ye have the poor always with you, but me ye have not always.' Ye can always do good to them, whenever you please." Why, He seems here to retort upon her accusers. "If there are any poor about, give to them yourselves; empty that bag of mine out, Judas; don't be hiding that away in your girdle. 'Whensoever *ye* will, ye may do them good.' Don't begin talking about the poor, and about what might have been done; go you, and do what might have been done yourselves; this poor woman hath done a good thing for me; I shall not be here long; don't trouble her." And so, beloved, if you murmur at men because they do not go in your ordinary ways, because they venture a little out of the regular line, there is plenty for you to do; your errands perhaps is not there exactly, but there is plenty for you to do, go and do it, and do not blame those who do extraordinary things. If you want subscribers to the guinea list, you can have them; it is those who give all they have, that are the varieties. Do not trouble those men. There are not many of them. They will not trouble you. You will have to travel from here to John o'Groat's house, before you knock against many dozen. They are rare creatures not often discovered. Do not trouble them; they may be fanatical, they may be excessive; but if you should build an asylum to put them all in, it would require but a very small sort of a house. Let them alone; there are not many who do much for their Master—not many who are irrational enough to think that there is nothing worth living for but to glorify Christ and magnify His holy name.

But the third excuse is the most extraordinary that could be given. Says Christ, "in that she poured this ointment on my body, she did it for my burial." What! did this woman forestall the Messiah's death? And had she the fond idea that, since no loving hand might embalm Him, she would anoint His sacred body by anticipation? Did her faith just then penetrate those deep shades of mystery about to be gradually unraveled? I think not. I think her love was more conspicuous than her faith. It strikes me that in these words we have rather the construction that Christ put upon her act. If so, the virtue of her action was derived from Him on whom it was wrought. "Your righteousness is of me," says the Lord. Sometimes when your heart prompts you to go and do such-and-such a thing for Christ, you cannot tell what you are doing. You may be doing a very simple thing in appearance, but there may be some wonderful, some matchless meaning in it. Christ may be but sending you, as it were, to take hold of one golden link—mayhap there are ten thousand will come after it. This woman thought she was just anointing Christ. "Nay," says Christ, "she is anointing me for my burial." There was more in her act than she knew of. And there is more in the spiritual promptings of our heart than we shall ever discover to the day of judgment. When first of all the Lord said to Whitfield, "Go and preach out on Kennington Common," did Whitfield know what was to be the result? No, he thought, doubtless, that he should just stand for once on the top of a table, and address some five thousand people. But there was a greater intent in the womb of Providence. The Lord meant that to see the whole country in a blaze, and to bring forth a glorious renewal of Pentecostal times, the like of which had not been seen before. Only seek to have your heart filled with love, and then obey its first spiritual dictate. Stop not. However extraordinary may be the mandate, go and do it. Have your wings outstretched like the angels before the throne, and the very moment that the echo vibrates in your heart, fly, fly, and you shall be flying you know not whither—you shall be upon an errand higher and nobler than your imagination has ever dreamed.

An Appeal Personally to You

Now I come to the conclusion, which is this—TO APPEAL PERSONALLY TO YOU, and ask you whether you know anything about the lesson which this woman's history is designed to teach.

Imagine your Savior, who has bought you with His blood, standing in this pulpit for a moment. He lifts up His hands, once rent with the nails, He exposes to you His side, pierced with a spear. Now picture Him. Lose sight of me for a moment, and see Him! And He puts to each one of you the question—"I suffered all this for you; what *have you* ever done for Me?" Answer Him now! Like honest followers of the Lamb of God, look back and see what you have ever done. You have gone up, you say, to His house. Was not that for your own profit? Did you do it for Him? You have contributed to His cause. Ah! you have, and some of you have done well in this thing; but think, how much have you given in proportion to what God has given to you? What have you done for Christ? Well, you have perhaps, some years ago, taught children for Him in the Sunday school, but it is all over; you have not been a Sunday school teacher these last many years. Jesus asks you, "What have you done for Me? In three years," He says, "I wrought out your redemption; in three years of agony, of toil, of suffering, I bought you with My blood; what have you done for Me in these ten, twenty, thirty years, since you knew My love, and tasted of My power to save?" Cover your faces, my friends, cover your faces. Let each man among us do so. Let us blush and weep. Lord Jesus! there was never such a friend as You are; but never were there such unfriendly ones as we are. Christ has some of the most ungrateful followers that man ever had. We have done little. If we have done much, we have done little. But some of you have done nothing at all for Christ.

That question answered, there comes another. I beseech you, let the vision of that crucified One stand before you. He says to you this morning, "What *will you* do for Me." Putting aside the past—you have wept over that, and blushed—what will you do now? Will you not now think of something that you can give Him, something that you can do for Him, something you can consecrate to Him? Come, you Marys, bring out your alabaster box! Come, you loving Johns, lift your heads for a moment from His bosom, and think of something that you can do for Him who lets you lean your head upon His heart. Come, come, you followers of Christ! Need I press you? Surely, if you needed it, my pressing would be in vain. But no; instinctively inspired by the Holy Spirit, you will each of you say, "Lord Jesus, from this day forth I desire to serve Thee better; but, Lord, tell me what you would have me to do." He does tell you now. I do not know what it is. The Spirit shall tell that to each one among you. But I do entreat you think not about it, but do it.

To the whole church of Christ I have one word to speak. I do feel—and I speak here of myself and of all Christians as in one mass—I do feel that the church of Christ in these days too much forgets her obligations to her Master. Oh! in the early church how did religion spread! It was because no man thought his life his own, or counted anything dear to him, so that he might win Christ, and be found in Him at last. Look how the ancient church, which was but a handful, within a century had stormed every known nation, and had carried the gospel throughout the length and breadth of the entire known world. But now we stay at home, penned up in England, or cooped up in America. We go not abroad where heathens dwell. Though we send here and there a man—one drafted as it were out of thousands; we do little or nothing for the evangelization of the world, and the sending forth of the ministers of the truth. Why, the early church, if it were here now, and we were gone, would within another fifty years sound the trumpet of the heavenly jubilee throughout the entire earth. With our means of traveling, with our appliances, with our books and helps, give such a church as the first Pentecostal one but fifty years, and the whole earth would be covered with the knowledge of the Lord, God the Holy Spirit going forth with them. But no, we cannot spend our lives for

Christ; we are not like the soldiers who marched to victory over the dead bodies of their brethren. We shall never sow the world with truth until it is sown with our blood again. "The blood of the martyrs is the seed of the church." I would that the church would burst forth from all her bonds, and send out her chosen warriors to do battle against the infidel hosts. And what if they should fall? What if they should die? With the Spirit of Christ inflaming our hearts, we should go forward, our courage nothing damped nor our ardor abated for all that—each one counting it an honor to die for Christ, each one throwing himself into the breach determined to win for Christ, and spread His name through the whole earth, or else to perish in the attempt. God give to His church this zeal and ardor; and then the time to favor Zion, yes her set time, shall have come.

5

*The Woman Who Was a Sinner**

And, behold, a woman in the city, which was a sinner, when she knew that Jesus sat at meat in the Pharisee's house, brought an alabaster box of ointment, and stood at his feet behind him weeping, and began to wash his feet with tears, and did wipe them with the hairs of her head, and kissed his feet, and anointed them with the ointment (Luke 7:37–38).

This is the woman who has been confounded with Mary Magdalene. How the error originated it would not be easy to imagine, but error it certainly is. There is not the slightest shadow of evidence that this woman, who was a sinner, had even the remotest connection with her out of whom Jesus cast seven devils. In delivering you a sermon a few Sunday ago upon the life of Mary Magdala, I think I showed you that it was hardly possible, and most improbable, that she could have been a sinner in the sense here intended, and now I venture to affirm that there is as much evidence to prove that the woman, in the narrative now before us, was the Queen of Sheba, or the mother of Sisera, as that she was Mary Magdalene: there is not a figment or fraction of evidence to be found. The fact is, there is no connection between the two.

Further, the sinner before us is not Mary of Bethany, with whom so many have confounded her. Mary, the sister of Martha and Lazarus, did anoint our Savior, but this is a previous anointing, by quite a different person, and the two narratives are altogether distinct. There is a great likeness, certainly, between the two. The principal persons were both women, full of ardent love to Christ; they both anointed the Lord with ointment; the name of Simon is connected with both, and they both wiped the Savior's

* This sermon was taken from *The Metropolitan Tabernacle Pulpit* and was preached on Sunday morning, March 22, 1868.

feet with their hair. But it ought not to astonish you that there were two persons whose intense affection thus displayed itself; the astonishment should rather be that there were not two hundred who did so, for the anointing of the feet of an honored friend was by no means so uncommon a token of respect among the Orientals as to be an unprecedented marvel. Loved as Jesus deserved to be, the marvel is that He was not oftener visited with these generous tokens of human love. It is a pity to fuse two occasions into one, as though we grudged a double unction to the Anointed of the Lord. That both events should happen in the houses of persons named Simon is not at all remarkable: be it remembered that the one was Simon the Pharisee, and the other Simon the leper; and that Simon is one of the most common Jewish names; and that in our days, a thing having happened in the house of a John, and another thing like it in the house of another John, would not be remarkable, since Johns are exceedingly common among us, as were Simons in the days of our Lord.

But that the two, or perhaps I should say three, anointings (for I am inclined to think there were three) are not the same is evident from the following reasons: they differ in time; our Lord lived at least six months after His anointing by this woman, and if you follow the narrative, you read in the very next chapter, "And it came to pass afterward, that he went throughout every city and village, preaching and shewing the glad tidings of the kingdom of God: and the twelve were with him." But when Mary anointed Him at Bethany, He said, "She did it for my burial"; and our Lord was within a very few days of His crucifixion. The anointing by Mary, the sister of Lazarus, took place at Bethany (Matt. 26:6), but this occurred in Galilee, which is quite another quarter. Moreover, the fact itself was really a very different one, for although both women anoint Christ with ointment, yet there was a peculiar preciousness and power of perfume about the spikenard of the wealthier Mary, which is not mentioned in the ointment of this woman of a lower position in life. Mary, according to John (John 12:3), poured out a whole pound of costly nard, but such is not said of the humble offering of the woman that was a sinner. Matthew tells us that a woman poured the ointment on His head, but this poor penitent is only said to have anointed His feet: tears are not mentioned in connection with Mary by either Matthew, Mark, or John, while they make a conspicuous feature in the love of the gracious mourner now before us.

After the transaction there was an objection raised in both cases, but mark the great difference! In this case, Simon the Pharisee objected because she, being a sinner, was allowed to have such familiarity with the Lord; in the other case, no such objection was raised to the person, but Judas Iscariot objected to her having been so profuse and extravagant in the abundance and costliness of the anointing, and murmured, saying that this ointment might have been sold for much and given to the poor. If you confound these two occurrences, you not only make an egregious mistake, but you lose a precious lesson. This case now before us is the offering of a poor returning wanderer, who, under a deep sense of gratitude, brings the best she has to her Lord, and is accepted by His grace. In the case of Mary of Bethany, it was an advanced saint, one who had sat at Jesus' feet and heard of Him, and had aforetime chosen the good part which should not be taken away from her, and she brings a costly tribute as the offering of her deep, sincere affection, which had grown and deepened by the receipt of many favors from His loving hand. The advanced believer is more bold than the new convert. She anoints His head when the other only anoints His feet, and she is not less loving, for if there be fewer tears there is a more costly spikenard. Jesus defended the penitent, and bade her go in peace; but in Mary's case there was no need to say, "Thy sins are forgiven," for she already possessed that priceless boon; our Lord, instead of merely defending, warmly eulogized her love, and declared, "Wheresoever this gospel shall be preached in the whole world, there shall also this, that this woman hath done, be told for a memorial of her." Thus much will suffice to show you that "the woman which was a sinner" is neither to be confounded with Mary of Magdala on the one hand, or Mary of Bethany on the other. Let us learn to read our Bibles with our eyes open, to study them as men do the works of great artists, studying each figure, and even each sweet variety of light and shade.

Too long have we been controverting on the threshold of the text, let us now lift the latch. Lo, on the table I see two savory dishes, let us feed thereon. Here are two silver bells, let us ring them; their notes are heavenly—O for ears to hear their rich, clear melody! The first note is *Grace*, and the second tone is *Love*.

Grace

GRACE, the most costly of spikenard: this story literally drips with it, like those Oriental trees which bleed perfume; or as the spouse when she rose up to open to her beloved, and her hands dropped with myrrh, and her fingers with sweet-smelling myrrh upon the handles of the lock. Grace, that gentle dew of heaven, is here plenteously distilled, and falls like small rain upon the tender herb. Grace, sovereign, distinguishing, omnipotent, is exceedingly magnified in this narrative; lo, I see it exalted upon a glorious high throne, with the king's daughter waiting as an honorable woman among its courtiers.

1. First, grace is here glorified *in its object*. She was "*a sinner*"—a sinner not in the flippant, unmeaning, everyday sense of the term, but a sinner in the blacker, filthier, and more obnoxious sense. She had forsaken the guide of her youth, and forgotten the covenant of her God; she had sinned against the laws of purity, and had made herself as a defiled thing; she had fallen into that deep ditch concerning which it is written, "The abhorred of

the Lord shall fall therein." According to our Lord's parable, she was in comparison with the Pharisee as a five-hundred-pence sinner, while the Pharisee was but as fifty. She was one of the scarlet sinners that we read of in Scripture—she sinned and made others to sin. Hers were offenses which provoke the Lord to jealousy, and stir up His wrath. Yet, oh, miracle of miracles, she was an object of distinguishing grace, ordained unto eternal life! Why was this? On what legal grounds was she selected? For what merit was she chosen? Was this an extraordinary and out-of-the-way instance? By no means, dear friends, for the grace of God has frequently chosen the lowest of the low, and the vilest of the vile. Recollect how, in the pedigree of our Lord, you find the name of the shameless Tamar, the harlot Rahab, and the unfaithful Bathsheba, as if to indicate that the Savior of sinners would enter into near relationship with the most degraded and fallen of our race. This is, in fact, one of the dearest titles of our Lord, though it was hissed at Him from the lips of contempt, "A friend of publicans and sinners." This is Jesus' character of which He is not ashamed: "This man receiveth sinners and eateth with them." Free grace has made no distinction among men on account of merit, whether false or real, if real there be. The law has concluded us all in unbelief, and then the abounding grace of God looking upon us all as equally cast away and ruined both by Adam's fall and by our own personal transgression, has predestinated and called whomsoever it would. Do you not hear from the throne of mercy the echoes of that sovereign proclamation, "I will have mercy on whom I will have mercy; I will have compassion on whom I will have compassion"? Grace has pitched upon the most unlikely cases in order to show itself to be grace; it has found a dwelling place for itself in the most unworthy hearts, that its freeness might be the better seen. Do I address one who has greatly fallen? Let this thought comfort you, if your heart bewails your sin—let this give you hope of mercy, that in the election of grace some of the grossest blasphemers, persecutors, thieves, fornicators, and drunkards, have been included, and in consequence thereof they have been forgiven, renewed, and made to live sober, righteous, and godly lives. Such as these have obtained mercy that in them first God might show forth all long-suffering as a comfort and encouragement to others to cry unto the Lord for mercy.

Grace reigns right majestically in the case before us, in that *this particular sinner* should be chosen; to choose a sinner was something, but to choose this one individual was even more astonishing. No doubt, she did in spirit ask herself, "Why me, Lord? why me?" Had she been here this morning, she would sing as heartily as any of us—

> Oh, gift of gifts! Oh, grace of faith!
> My God, how can it be

That thou, who hast discerning love,
Shouldst give that gift to me!

How many hearts thou mightst have had
More innocent than mine!
How many souls more worthy far
Of that pure touch of thine!

Ah, Grace! into unlikeliest hearts
It is thy boast to come;
The glory of thy light to find
In darkest spots a home.

At yonder table sits Simon the Pharisee, a good respectable body as he thinks himself to be, and yet no choice divine has fallen upon him—while this poor harlot is elected by distinguishing grace! How can we account for this? Many there were in the city like to herself, some worse, some better; but grace had marked her as its own. Oh, strange, yet admirable sovereignty! Now, it is possible that you may not be much taken with the glory of grace in selecting her, but I will ask you whether you are not delighted with the grace which separated *you* to be the Lord's? O brethren, when once a man discovers that God has chosen him, when he feels that grace has broken his heart, has brought him to Christ, and has covered him with a perfect righteousness, then he breaks out in wondering exclamations, "How could you have chosen me? What am I, and what is my father's house, that I should be taken into such royal favor?" The more a believer looks within, the more he discovers reasons for divine wrath, and the less he believes in his own personal merit. How is the heart of a true believer filled with adoring gratitude that ever the Lord's boundless love should have been pleased to settle and fix itself upon Him! This is not so much for me to descant upon as it is for your private meditations. I earnestly commend to you that precious thought, that Jehovah loved you from before the foundations of the world, and chose you when He might have left you, chose you when He passed over thousands of the great and the noble, the wise, and the learned. The doctrine is not a dogma to be fought over, as dogs over a bone, but to be rejoiced in, and turned to practical account as an incentive to reverent wonder and affectionate gratitude. Where sin abounded grace did much more abound, and the "woman which was a sinner," is now before us a weeping penitent; the sinner "of the city," a public sinner, is now openly a follower of the holy One.

2. Grace is greatly magnified in *its fruits*. Who would have thought that a woman who had yielded her members to be servants of unrighteousness, to her shame and confusion, should have now become, what if I call her a maid of honor to the King of kings?—one of Christ's most favored servi-

tors? Who offered hospitalities to Jesus which the Pharisee omitted, and offered them in an infinitely better spirit and style than the Pharisee could have done it even had he tried! Let us remark, that the grace of God brought this woman in a way of providence to listen to the Savior's discourses. In a former part of this chapter it appears He had been preaching the gospel, and more especially preaching it to the poor. Perhaps she stood in the street attracted by the crowd, and, as she listened to our Savior's talk, it seemed to hold her fast. She had never heard a man speak after that fashion, and when He spoke of abounding mercy, and the willingness of God to accept as many as would come to Him, then the tears began to follow each other down her cheek; and when she listened again to that meek and lowly preacher, and heard Him tell of the Father in heaven who would receive prodigals and press them to His loving bosom, then her heart was fairly broken, she relinquished her evil traffic, she became a new woman, desirous of better things, anxious to be freed from sin. But she was greatly agitated in her heart with the question, could she, be really forgiven? Would such pardoning love as she had heard of reach even to her? She hoped so, and was in a measure comforted. Her faith grew, and with it an ardent love. The Spirit of God still wrought with her until she enjoyed a feeble hope, a gleam of confidence; she believed that Jesus of Nazareth was the Messiah, that He had appeared on earth to forgive sins, and she rested on Him for the forgiveness of her sins, and longed for an opportunity to do Him homage, and if possible to win a word direct from His mouth. The Lord of mercy came to the city where she lived. "Now," she thought, "here is my opportunity; that blessed Prophet has come; the Man who spoke as never man spoke is near me, and I have already derived such benefit from Him that I love Him better than all besides; I love Him as my own soul. I will steal into the house of the Pharisee, that I may feast my eyes with the sight of Him." Now, when she came to the door, the Savior was reclining at His meat, according to the Oriental custom, and His feet were toward the door: for the Pharisee had but little respect for Christ, and had not given Him the best and innermost place at the feast; but there He lay with His uncovered feet toward the door, and the woman, almost unperceived, came close to Him, and, as she looked and saw that the Pharisee had refused Him the ordinary courtesy of washing His feet, and that they were all stained and travel-worn with His long journeys of love, she began to weep, and the tears fell in such plenteous showers that they even washed His feet. Here was holy water of a true sort. The crystal of penitence falling in drops, each one as precious as a diamond. Never were feet bedewed with a more precious water than those penitent eyes showered forth. Then, unbinding those luxurious tresses, which had been for her the devil's nets in which to entangle souls, she wiped the sacred feet therewith. Surely she thought that her chief adornment, the crown and glory of her womanhood, was all too worthless a thing to do service to the lowest and meanest part of the Son of God. That which once was her vanity now was humbled and yet exalted to the lowest office; she made her eyes a ewer and her locks a towel. "Never," says Bishop Hall, "was any hair so preferred as this; how I envy those locks that were graced with the touch of those sacred feet."

There a sweet temptation overtook her, "I will even kiss those feet, I will humbly pay reverence to those blessed limbs." She spoke not a word, but how eloquent were her actions! Better even than psalms and hymns were these acts of devotion. Then she bethought her of that alabaster box containing perfumed oil with which, like most Eastern women, she was wont to anoint herself for the pleasure of smell and for the increase of her beauty, and now, opening it, she pours out the costliest things she has upon His blessed feet. Not a word, I say, came from her; and, brethren, we would prefer a single speechless love of Jesus, who acted as she did, to ten thousand noisy talkers who have no gifts, no heart, no tears. As for the Master, He remained quietly acquiescent, saying nothing, but all the while drinking in her love, and letting His poor weary heart find sweet solace in the gratitude of one who once *was* a sinner, but who was to be such no more.

Grace, my brethren, deserves our praise, since it does so much for its object. Grace does not choose a man and leave him as he is. My brethren and sisters, men rail at grace sometimes as though it were opposed to morality, whereas it is the great source and cause of all complete morality—indeed, there is no real holiness in the sight of God except that which grace creates, and which grace sustains. This woman, apart from grace, had remained black and defiled still to her dying day, but the grace of God wrought a wondrous transformation, removing the impudence of her face, the flattery from her lips, the finery from her dress, and the lust from her heart. Eyes which were full of adultery, were now founts of repentance; lips which were doors of lascivious speech, now yield holy kisses—the profligate was a penitent, the castaway a new creature. All the actions which are attributed to this woman illustrate the transforming power of divine grace. She exhibited the deepest repentance. She wept abundantly. She wept out of no mere sentimentalism, but at the remembrance of her many crimes. She wept for sorrow and for shame as she thought over her early childhood, and how she had slighted a mother's training, how she had listened to the tempter's voice, and hurried on from bad to worse. Every part of her life story would rise before her as a painfully vivid dream. The sight of those blessed feet helped her to remember the dangerous path into which she had wandered; the sluices of grief were drawn up, and her soul flowed out in tears. O blessed Spirit of grace, we adore You as we see the rock smitten and the waters gushing. "He causes His wind to blow and the waters to flow."

Note the woman's humility. She had once possessed a brazen face, and knew no bashfulness, but now she stands behind the Savior. She did not push herself in before His face; she was content to have the meanest standing place. If she might not venture to anoint His head, yet, if she might do service to His feet, she blushed as she accepted the honor. Those who serve the Lord Jesus truly, have a holy bashfulness, a shrinking sense of their own unworthiness, and are content to fulfill the very lowest office in His household. That is no service for Christ when you would need ride the king's horse, and wear the king's garment, and have it said, "This is the man whom the king delighteth to honor." That is serving yourself rather than Christ, when you covet the chief place in the synagogue, and would have men call you Rabbi. But that is real service when you can care for the poor; when you can condescend to men of low estate, and become a teacher of the ignorant and an instructor of babes. He serves well who works behind His master's back, unknown and unperceived—toiling in the dark, unreported, unapplauded, and happy to have it so. See, beloved, how in a woman who was once so shameless, grace plants and makes to flourish the fair and modest flower of true humility.

Yet was the woman *courageous*, for she must have needed much courage to enter into a Pharisee's house. The look of a Pharisee to this woman must have been enough to freeze summer into howling winter. Those Pharisees had an insufferable contempt of everybody who was not of their own clique, who did not fast twice a week, and tithe their mint, anise, and cumin; they said, by every gesture, "Stand by, I am holier than thou." To a person of infamous character, the pompous Pharisee would be doubly contemptuous, and a woman conscious of unworthiness would be sorely wounded by his manners; besides, at a feast, her tears would be much out of place, and therefore she would be the more rudely rebuked; but how fearless she was, and how bravely she held her tongue when Simon railed! What will not men and women do when grace moves them to love, and love prompts them to courage! Ay, into the very jaws of hell the grace of God would make a believer dare to enter, if God commanded him. There is no mountain too high for a believing foot to scale, and no furnace too hot for a believing heart to bear. Let Rome and its amphitheaters, Piedmont and its snow, France and its galleys, Smithfield and its stakes, the Netherlands and their rivers of blood, all speak of what grace can do when once it reigns in the heart, what heroes it can make of the very weakest and most timid of God's children, where it rules supreme.

I have said that in every part of this woman's action grace is honored, and it is so more especially in this respect, that what she did was *practical*. Hers was not pretense, but real and expensive service. The religion of some professors stops short at their substance; it costs them nothing, and, I fear, is worth nothing. They appear before the Lord empty. They buy no sweet cane with money, neither does the Lord receive the fat of their sacrifices. I must confess myself utterly at a loss to understand the piety of some people. I thank God I am not bound to understand it, and that I am not sent into the world to be a judge of my fellow creatures, but I do greatly wonder at the religion of many. There are to be found, and I have found them, persons whose love to Christ is of such a sort that they give to His cause the larger proportion of their substance, and do so gladly, thinking it a privilege; yea, I know some who pinch themselves—some of the poor and needy, who stint themselves that they may give to Christ. Such are doubtless blessed in the deed. I do not understand those men who have thousands upon thousands of pounds, perhaps hundreds of thousands, and profess to love Christ, and dole out their gifts to Jesus in miserable fragments. I must leave them to their Master, to be judged at the last, but I confess I do not understand them or admire them. If I did love Christ at all, I would love Him so that I would give Him all I could, and if I did not do that, I think I would say, "He is not worth it, and I will not be a sham professor. It is rank hypocrisy to profess love and then to act a miserly part. Let those who are guilty of it settle the account between God and their own souls. This woman's alabaster box was given freely, and if she had had more to give, she would have given it, after the spirit of that other woman, that memorable widow, who had two mites, which made a farthing, which were all her living, but she gave it all out of love to God. Grace reigns indeed with high control when it leads men who naturally would be selfish to practice liberality in the cause of the Redeemer. Let these gleanings suffice, the vintage of the fruits of grace is too great for us to gather it all this morning.

3. I would have you remark, in the third place, that grace is seen by attentive eyes in *our Lord's acceptance* of what this chosen vessel had to bring. Jesus knew her sin. The Pharisee wondered that Jesus did not shrink from contact with her. You and I may wonder too. We sometimes feel it a task to have to commune with persons of a certain character even when they profess to repent: our Lord's sensitiveness of the guilt of sin was much keener than ours, yet He rested still upon the couch, and quietly accepted what she brought, permitted her the fond familiarity of kissing His feet again and again, and to bedew them with her tears—permitted all that, I say, and accepted all that, and herein made His grace to shine most brightly. Oh, that Jesus should ever accept anything of me, that He should be willing to accept my tears, willing to receive my prayers and my praises! We cheerfully accept a little flower from a child, but then the flower is beautiful, and we are not far above the child, but Jesus accepts from us that which is in its nature impure, and upbraids us not. O grace, how condescending you are; see, believer, Jesus has heard your prayers and answered them; He has blessed your labors, given you souls as your reward, and at this moment that which is in your heart to do for Him He

receives, and He raises no objection, but takes what you bring to Him, takes it with joy. O grace, you are grace indeed, when the offerings of unworthy ones become dear unto Jesus' heart.

4. Further, grace is displayed in this narrative when you see *our Lord Jesus Christ become the defender of the penitent.* Everywhere grace is the object of human cavil: men snap at it like evening wolves. Some attack it at the fountain head; they cannot endure the doctrine of election. Some professors almost foam at the mouth at the very mention of the word "predestination"; they cannot bear it, and yet it is God's truth, let them say what they will, and there shall it stand, let them kick against the pricks if they dare. "It is not of him that willeth, nor of him that runneth, but of God that sheweth mercy." Would to God men would give up their rebellious questionings and bow before the King of kings. On this occasion, Simon caviled at grace in its objects, its condescension, its generosity, its tenderness; he was angry that a sinful woman should be allowed to approach the Lord, he would have put her in quarantine at the least, if not in prison. Some object to grace in its perpetuity, they struggle against persevering grace; but others, like this Simon, struggle against the bounty of grace. How could such a woman as she be permitted to draw so near to Christ? Certain captious spirits will demand, "How should Jesus give to such unworthy ones such acceptance, such manifestations of Himself, such privileges?" Our Lord took upon Himself to defend her, and therefore she might well afford to hold her tongue. So shall it be with you. If Satan accuse you, and your enemies with loud-mouthed accusations cry out against you, you have an advocate with the Father, Jesus Christ the righteous, who will certainly plead your cause and clear you. Jesus by His defensive parable shows that He was justified in letting the woman approach, because great love prompted her. There was no sin in her approach, but much to commend, since her motive was excellent, and the motive is the true measure of a deed. She felt intense love and gratitude toward the person who had forgiven her; therefore, her acts were not to be forbidden, but commended. He justifies her and incidentally justifies Himself. Had He not done well in having won a sinner's heart to penitence and love? Was not election justified in having chosen one to such holy devotedness and fervency? At the last great day, the Lord will justify His grace before the eyes of the whole universe, for He will allow the grace-wrought virtues of His chosen ones to be unveiled, and all eyes shall see that grace reigns through righteousness. Then shall they forever be silenced who accused the grace of God of leading to licentiousness, for they shall see that in every case free forgiveness led to gratitude and gratitude to holiness. The chosen shall be made choice men. Grace chose them notwithstanding all their deformities; but when it has cast about them a supernal beauty, they shall be the wonder and admiration of the universe, evidently made to be the noblest and best of mankind. Show me where

grace ever created sin! You cannot, but lo, in what a manner has grace created holiness! It is not ashamed to let its chosen sheep appear before the great dividing Shepherd's throne, for of them all it shall be said, "Come, ye blessed of my Father, inherit the kingdom prepared for you from the foundation of the world: for I was an hungered, and ye gave me meat: I was thirsty, and ye gave me drink." Grace does not smuggle men into heaven, but brings them up to heaven's requirements through the Spirit and the blood.

5. Once more, my brethren, the grace of God is seen in this narrative in *the bestowal of yet richer favors*. Great grace saved her, rich grace encouraged her, unbounded grace gave her a divine assurance of forgiveness. It was proved that she was forgiven, for she loved much, but she had never received the full assurance of it. She was a hopeful penitent rather than a confirmed believer. But the Master said, "Thy sins are forgiven thee"; from that moment full assurance of faith must have occupied her soul. And then He gave her that choice dismissary benediction, "Go in peace," by which the peace of God which passseth all understanding henceforth kept her mind, so that even when she had to go out of this world into the unknown realm, she heard in the midst of Jordan's billows, the divine sentence, "Go in peace." Ah! beloved, you know not what grace can do for you. God is not stinted in His grace. If He has lifted you up out of the miry clay, He can do more, He can set your feet upon a rock. If on the rock you already stand, He can do more, He can put a new song into your mouth; and if already you lift the joyous hymn, He can do more yet, He can establish your goings. You do not know the exceeding bounty of your own heavenly Father yet. Unfathomable is His goodness. Arise and enjoy it. Behold the whole land is before you, from Dan unto Beersheba—all the provisions of the covenant of grace belong to you. Have but faith, and you shall yet comprehend with all saints what are the heights and depths, and know the love of Christ which passes knowledge.

Here then, was grace in its object, grace in its fruit, grace in the acceptance of that fruit, grace in the defense which Jesus made of the gracious one, and grace in the blessings bestowed upon her. May grace deal thus bountifully with us.

Love

We have but two or three moments left for what requires far more space, namely, LOVE. The word blossoms with roses, and suggests the voice of the turtle and the singing of birds. Our time, however, binds us to a narrow path, which we must not leave, although the beds of lilies on either hand invite us.

Love—its source: it bubbles up as a pure rill from the well-head of grace. She loved much, but it was because much had been forgiven. There is no such thing as mere natural love to God. The only true love which can burn in the human breast toward the Lord, is that which the Holy Spirit Himself kindles. If you truly love the God who made you and redeemed you, you may be well assured that you are His child, for none but His children have any love to Him.

Its *secondary cause* is faith. The fiftieth verse tells us, "Thy faith hath saved thee." Our souls do not begin with loving Christ, but the first lesson is to trust. Many penitents attempt this difficult task; they aspire to reach the stair-head without treading the steps; they would needs be at the pinnacle of the temple before they have crossed the threshold. First trust Christ for the pardon of your sin: when you have done this, your sins are forgiven, and then love shall flash to your heart as the result of gratitude for what the Redeemer has done for you. Grace is the source of love, but faith is the agent by which love is brought to us.

The food of love is a sense of sin, and a grateful sense of forgiveness. If you and I felt more deeply the guilt of our past lives, we should love Jesus Christ better. If we had but a clearer sense that our sins deserve the deepest hell, that Christ suffered what we ought to have suffered in order to redeem us from our iniquities, we should not be such cold-hearted creatures as we are. We are perfectly monstrous in our want of love to Christ, but the true secret of it is a forgetfulness of our ruined and lost natural estate, and a forgetfulness of the sufferings of which we have been redeemed from that condition. O that our love might feed itself this day, and find a renewal of its strength in remembering what sovereign grace has done.

Love in the narrative before us shines in the fact that the service the woman rendered to our Lord was perfectly voluntary. No one suggested it, much less pressed it upon her. It takes the gloss off our service when we need to be dragged to it, or pushed forward by some energetic pleader. Brethren, the anointing was impromptu with her. Christ was there, and it was at her own suggestion that she anointed His feet. Mary of Bethany had not then set the example: the woman who was a sinner was an original in her service. In these days we have many inventors and discoverers for our temporal use and service, why should we not have inventors for Jesus who will bring out new projects of usefulness? We are most of us content to travel in the old rut, but if we had more love to Jesus we should be more eccentric, and should have a degree of freshness about our service which at present is all too rare. Lord, give us the love which can lead the way!

Her service to Jesus was *personal*. She did it all herself, and all *to Him*. Do you notice how many times the pronoun occurs in our text? "She stood at *his* feet behind *him* weeping, and began to wash *his* feet with tears, and did wipe *them* with the hairs of her head, and kissed *his* feet, and anointed *them* with the ointment." She served Christ Himself. It was neither service to Peter, nor James, nor John, nor yet to the poor or sick of the city, but to the Master Himself; and, depend upon it, when our love is in active exercise, our piety will be immediately toward Christ—we shall sing to Him, pray to Him, teach for Him, preach for Him, live to Him. Forgetfulness of the personality of Christ takes away the very vitality of our religion. How much better will you teach, this afternoon, in your Sunday school class, if you teach your children for Christ! How much better will you go forth this evening to tell to others the way of salvation, if you go to do it for His sake! Then you court no man's smile—you fear no man's frown. It is enough for you that you have done it for the Master, and if the Master accepts it you have the reward in that very fact.

The woman's service showed her love in that it was *fervent*. There was so much affection in it—nothing conventional; no following chilly propriety, no hesitating inquiry for precedents. Why did she kiss His feet? Was it not a superfluity? What was the good of it? Did it not look sentimental, affected, sensuous, indelicate? Little did she care how it looked; she knew what she meant. She could not do otherwise. Her whole soul went out in love, she acted naturally as her heart dictated, and, brethren, she acted well. O for more of this guileless piety, which hurls decorum and regulation to the winds. Ah, throw your souls into the service of Christ; let your heart burn in His presence, and let all your soul belong to Jesus. Serve not your Master as though you were half asleep, do not work with drooping hands and half-closed eyes, but wake up the whole of your powers and passions: for such love as He has shown to you, give the most awakened and quickened love in return. O for more of this love! If I might only pray one prayer this morning, I think it should be that the flaming torch of the love of Jesus should be brought into everyone of our hearts, and that all our passions should be set ablaze with love to Him.

One thought more, and I have done. This woman's love is a lesson to us in *the opportunity* which she seized. She was evidently but just pardoned: she was rather a weeper than one who had learned to rejoice, and yet for all that, she would serve Him at the first dawn of her spiritual life. Now, you young converts, no longer say, "We will do something for Christ in a few years' time, when we have made our calling and election sure; we will wait until we have grown in grace, and then try to do what we can." No, no, but as soon as you are washed, bring your offering to Jesus. The very day of your conversion, enlist in His army, for speedy obedience is beautiful. Perhaps if this woman had lingered, she had never anointed the Lord at all; but in the hot flush of her first love, she did well to perform at once this zealous, fervent act. Young converts maintain, by God's grace, the warmth of the blood which circulates in the church's veins. Old churches generally become diseased churches when they cease to grow. I do not know a church in all England without conversions which is at all in a happy spiritual state. The fact is, the fresh comers stir us all up by their fervor, their simplicity, their childlike confidence. Now, beloved ones, we encourage you to show this. For our sakes, for your own sakes, for Christ's sake, do not hesitate—if there be anything you can do, though you are uneducated in the divine school, do it. Though there may be a dozen blunders in the method, yet do it, for Christ will accept it. The Pharisee may cavil—well, perhaps it may keep his tongue from other mischief—let him cavil, you can bear it, Christ *will* defend you, Jesus will accept you; and as a reward for doing what you can, He may be pleased to give you grace to do more, and may breathe over you a full assurance of faith, which had you been idle you might not for years have attained; and He may give you a peace of conscience in serving Him which, had you sat still, might never have come to you. I beseech all of you who love Jesus, do not hide the light you have under a bushel, but come out and show it. If you have but a little faith, use it; if you have only a grain of faith, turn it to account. Put the one talent out at interest, and use it for the Master at once, and the Lord bless you in such a work, by increasing your faith and love, and making you to be as this woman was, a highly favored servant of this blessed Master. May the Lord give everyone of you His blessing for Jesus' sake.

6

*The Little Dogs**

But he answered and said, It is not meet to take the children's bread, and to cast it to dogs. And she said, Truth, Lord: yet the dogs eat of the crumbs which fall from their masters' table (Matthew 15:26–27).

But Jesus said unto her, Let the children first be filled: for it is not meet to take the children's bread, and to cast it unto the dogs. And she answered and said unto him, Yes, Lord: yet the dogs under the table eat of the children's crumbs (Mark 7:27–28).

I take the two records of Matthew and Mark that we may have the whole matter before us. May the Holy Spirit bless our meditations thereon.

The brightest jewels are often found in the darkest places. Christ had not found such faith, no, not in Israel, as He discovered in this poor Canaanitish woman. The borders and fringes of the land were more fruitful than the center, where the husbandry had been more abundant. In the headlands of the field, where the farmer does not expect to grow much beyond weeds, the Lord Jesus found the richest ear of corn that as yet had filled His sheaf. Let those of us who reap after Him be encouraged to expect the same experience. Never let us speak of any district as too depraved to yield us converts, nor of any class of persons as too fallen to become believers. Let us go even to the borders of Tyre and Sidon, though the land be under a curse, for even there we shall discover some elect one, ordained to be a jewel for the Redeemer's crown. Our heavenly Father has children everywhere.

In spiritual things it is found that the best plants often grow in the most barren soil. Solomon spoke of trees, and discoursed concerning the hyssop on the wall and the cedar in Lebanon. So is it in the natural world, the great trees are found on great mountains and the minor plants in places adapt-

* This sermon was taken from *The Metropolitan Tabernacle Pulpit* and was preached on Sunday morning, August 6, 1876.

ed for their tiny roots but it is not so among the plants of the Lord's right hand planting, for there we have seen the cedar grow upon the wall—great saints in places where it was apparently impossible for them to exist; and we have seen hyssops growing upon Lebanon—a questionable, insignificant piety, where there have been innumerable advantages. The Lord is able to make strong faith exist with little knowledge, little present enjoyment and little encouragement; and strong faith in such conditions triumphs and conquers, and doubly glorifies the grace of God. Such was this Canaanitish woman, a cedar growing where soil was scant enough. She was a woman of amazing faith, though she could have heard but little of Him in whom she believed, and perhaps had never seen His person at all until the day when she fell at His feet and said, "Lord, help me!"

Our Lord had a very quick eye for spying faith. If the jewel was lying in the mire His eye caught its glitter, if there was a choice ear of wheat among the thorns He failed not to perceive it. Faith has a strong attraction for the Lord Jesus; at the sight of it "the king is held in the galleries" and cries "thou hast ravished my heart with one of thine eyes, with one chain of thy neck." The Lord Jesus was charmed with the fair jewel of this woman's faith, and watching it and delighting in it He resolved to turn it around and set it in other lights, that the various facets of this priceless diamond might each one flash its brilliance and delight His soul. Therefore He tried her faith by His silence, and by His discouraging replies, that He might see its strength; but He was all the while delighting in it, and secretly sustaining it, and when He had sufficiently tried it, He brought it forth as gold, and set His own royal mark upon it in these memorable words, "O woman, great is thy faith; be it unto thee even as thou wilt."

I am hopeful this morning that perhaps some poor soul in this place under very discouraging circumstances may nevertheless be led to believe in the Lord Jesus Christ with a strong and persevering faith, and though as yet it enjoys no peace, and has seen no gracious answer to prayer, I trust that its struggling faith may be strengthened this morning by the example of the Canaanitish woman.

I gather from the story of her appeal to the Lord Jesus and her success therein, four facts. The first is, *faith's mouth cannot be closed*; the second is, *faith never disputes with God*; thirdly, I perceive that *faith argues mightily*; and fourthly, that *faith wins her suit*.

The Mouth of Faith Can Never Be Closed

THE MOUTH OF FAITH CAN NEVER BE CLOSED; for if ever the faith of a woman was tried so as to make her cease from prayer, it was that of this daughter of Tyre. She had difficulty after difficulty to encounter, and yet she could not be put off from pleading for her little daughter, because she believed in Jesus as the great Messiah, able to heal all manner of diseases, and she meant to pray to Him until He yielded to her importunity, for she was confident that He could chase the demon from her child.

Observe that *the mouth of faith cannot be closed even on account of the closed ear and the closed mouth of Christ.* He answered her never a word. She spoke very piteously, she came and threw herself at His feet, her child's case was very urgent, her motherly heart was very tender, and her cries were very piercing, and yet He answered her never a word as if He were deaf and dumb, He passed her by; yet was she not staggered; she believed in Him, and even He Himself could not make her doubt Him, let Him try silence even if He would. It is hard to believe when prayer seems to be a failure. I would to God that some poor seeker here might believe that Jesus Christ is able and willing to save, and so fully believe it that his unanswered prayers shall not be able to make him doubt. Even if you should pray in vain by the month together, do not allow a doubt about the Lord Jesus and His power to save to cross your mind. What if you cannot yet grasp the peace which faith must ultimately bring you, what if you have no certainty of forgiveness of your sin, what if no gleams of joy should visit your spirit, yet believe you Him, who cannot lie. "Though he slay me," said Job, "yet will I trust in him." That was splendid faith. It would be a great deal for some if they could say, "Though he smite me, yet will I trust him," but Job said, "Though he slay me." If He put on the garb of an executioner, and come out against me as though He would destroy me, yet will I believe Him to be full of love: He is good and gracious still, I cannot doubt it, and therefore at His feet I will lie down and look up, expecting grace at His hands. Oh for such faith as this! O soul, if you have it, you are a saved man, as sure as you are alive. If even the Lord's apparent refusal to bless you cannot close your mouth, your faith is of a noble sort, and salvation is yours.

In the next place, *her faith could not be silenced by the conduct of the disciples.* They did not treat her well, but yet perhaps not altogether ill. They were not like their Master, but frequently repulsed those who would come to Him. Her noise annoyed them, she kept to them with boundless perseverance, and therefore they said, "Send her away, for she crieth *after us.*" Poor soul, she never cried after *them*, it was after their Master. Sometimes disciples become very important in their own eyes, and think that the pushing and crowding to hear the gospel is caused by the people's eagerness to hear *them*, whereas nobody would care for their poor talk if it were not for the gospel message which they are charged to deliver. Give us any other theme, and the multitude would soon melt away. Though weary of the woman's importunate cries, they acted somewhat kindly toward her, for they were evidently desirous that she should obtain the boon she sought, or else our Lord's reply would not have been appropriate, "I am not sent, save to the lost sheep of the house of Israel." It was not her daughter's healing that they cared for, but they consulted their own comfort, for they were anxious to be rid of her. "Send her away," said they, "for she crieth after us." Still, though they did not treat her as men should treat a woman, as disciples should treat a seeker, as Christians should treat everybody, yet for all that, her mouth was not stopped. Peter, I have no doubt, looked in a very scowling manner, and perhaps even John became a little impatient, for he had a quick temper by nature; Andrew and Philip and the rest of them considered her very impertinent and presumptuous; but she thought of her little daughter at home, and of the horrible miseries to which the demon subjected her, and so she pressed up to the Savior's feet and said, "Lord, help me." Cold, hard words and unkind, unsympathetic behavior could not prevent her pleading with Him in whom she believed. Ah, poor sinner, perhaps you are saying, " I am longing to be saved, but such and such a good Christian man has dealt very bitterly with me, he has doubted my sincerity and questioned the reality of my repentance, and caused me the deepest sorrow; it seems as if he did not wish me to be saved." Ah, dear friend, this is very trying, but if you have true faith in the Master you will not mind us disciples, neither the gentlest of us, nor the most crooked of us, but just urge on your suit with your Lord until He deigns to give you an answer of peace.

Her mouth, again, was not closed by exclusive doctrine, which appeared to confine the blessing to a favored few: the Lord Jesus Christ said, "I am not sent, save to the lost sheep of the house of Israel," and though properly understood there is nothing very severe in it, yet sentence must have fallen on the woman's heart like a talent of lead. "Alas," she might have thought, "then He is not sent to me; vainly do I seek for that which He reserves for the Jews." Now, the doctrine of election, which is assuredly taught in Scripture, ought not to hinder any soul from coming to Christ, for, if properly understood, it would rather encourage than discourage; and yet often to the uninstructed ear the doctrine of the divine choice of a people from before the foundation of world acts with very depressing effect. We have known poor seekers mournfully say, "Perhaps there is no mercy for me; I may be among those for whom no purpose of mercy has been formed." They have been tempted to cease from prayer for fear they should not have predestinated unto eternal life. Ah, dear soul, if you have the faith of God's elect in you, you will not be kept back by any self-condemning inferences drawn from the secret things of God, but you will believe in that which has been clearly revealed, and you will be assured that this cannot contradict the secret decrees of heaven. What though our Lord was only sent to the house of Israel, yet there is a house of Israel not after the flesh but after the spirit, and therefore the Syrophoenecian woman was included even where she thought she was shut out, and you may also be comprehended within those lines of gracious destiny which now distress you. At any rate, say to yourself, "In the election of grace others are included who were as sinful as I have been, why should not I? Others have been included who were as full of distress as I have been on account of sin, and why should not I be also?" Reasoning thus you will press forward; in hope believing against hope, suffering no plausible deduction from the doctrine of Scripture to prevent your believing in the appointed Redeemer.

The mouth of faith in this case was not even closed by a sense of admitted unworthiness. Christ spoke of dogs: He meant that the Gentiles were to Israel as the dogs: she did not at all dispute it, but yielded the point by saying, "Truth, Lord." She felt she was only worthy to be compared to a dog. I have no doubt her sense of unworthiness was very deep. She did not expect to win the boon she sought for on count of any merit of her own; she depended upon the goodness of Christ's heart, not on the goodness of her cause, and upon the excellence of His power rather than upon the prevalence of her plea; yet conscious as she was that she was only a poor Gentile dog, her prayers were not hindered; she cried, notwithstanding all, "Lord, help me." O sinner, if you feel yourself to be the worst sinner out of hell, still pray, believingly pray for mercy. If your sense of unworthiness be enough to drive you to self-destruction, yet I beseech you, out of the depths, out of the dungeon of self-loathing, still cry unto God; for your salvation rests in no measure or degree upon yourself, or upon anything that you are or have been or can be. You need to be saved *from* yourself, not *by* yourself. It is thine to be empty that Jesus may fill you; thine to confess your filthiness that He may wash you; thine to be less than nothing that Jesus may be everything to you. Suffer not the number, blackness, frequency, or heinousness of your transgressions to silence your prayers, but though you be a dog, yea not worthy to be set with the dogs of the Lord's flock, yet open your mouth in believing prayer.

There was beside this a general tone and spirit in what the Lord Jesus said which tended to depress the woman's hope and restrain her prayer, yet *she was not kept back by the darkest and most depressing influences.* "It is not meet," said the Lord Jesus, "it is not becoming, is not proper, it is hardly lawful, to take children's bread and throw it to dogs." Perhaps she did not quite see all that He might have meant, but what she did see was enough to pour cold water upon the flame of her hope, yet her faith was not quenched. It was a faith of that immortal kind which nothing can kill; for her mind was made up that whatever Jesus meant, or did not mean, she would not cease to trust Him, and urge her suit with Him. There are a great many things in and around the gospel which men see as in a haze, and being misunderstood they rather repel than attract seeking souls; but be they what they may we must resolve to come to Jesus at all risks. "If I perish, I perish." Beside the great stumbling-stone of election there are truths and facts which seekers magnify and misconstrue until they see a thousand difficulties. They are troubled about Christian experience, about being born again, about inbred sin, and all sorts of things; in fact, a thousand lions are in the way when the soul attempts to come to Jesus, but he who gives Christ the faith which He deserves says, "I fear none of these things. Lord, help me, and I will still confide in You. I will approach You. I will press through obstacles to You, and throw myself at Your dear feet, knowing that him that comes to You, You will in no wise cast out."

Faith Never Disputes with the Lord

Faith worships. You notice how Matthew says, "Then came she and worshiped him." Faith also begs and prays. You observe how Mark says, "She besought Him." She cried, "Lord, help me," after having said, "Have mercy on me, O Lord, thou Son of David." Faith pleads, but never disputes, not even against the hardest thing that Jesus says. If faith disputed—I am uttering a solecism—she would not be faith, for that which disputes is unbelief. Faith in God implies agreement with what God says, and consequently it excludes the idea of doubt. Genuine faith believes anything and everything the Lord says whether discouraging or encouraging. She never has a "but" or an "if," or even a "yet" to put in, but she stands to it, "You have said it, Lord, and therefore it is true: You have ordained it Lord, and therefore it is right." She never goes beyond that.

Observe in our text that *faith assents to all the Lord says.* She said, "Truth, Lord." What had He said? "You are comparable to a dog!" "Truth, Lord; truth, Lord; so I am." "It would not be meet that the children should be robbed of bread in order to feed dogs." "Truth Lord, it would not be fitting, and I would not have one of Your children deprived of grace for me." "It is not your time yet," said Jesus; "the children must *first* be fed; children at the meal times and dogs after dinner; this is Israel's time, and the Gentiles may follow after. But not yet." She virtually replies, "I know it, Lord, and agree thereto."

She does not raise a question or dispute the justice of the Lord's dispensing His own grace according to His sovereign good pleasure. She fails not, as some do who cavil at divine sovereignty. It would have proved that she had little or no faith if she had done that. She disputes not as to the Lord's set time and order. Jesus said, "Let the children first be filled," and she does not dispute the time, as many do, who will not have it that now is the accepted time, but are as much for postponing as this woman was for antedating the day of grace. She entered into no argument against its being improper to take the covenant bread from the children and give it to the uncircumcised heathen: she never wished Israel to be robbed for her. Dog as she was she would not have any purpose of God nor any propriety of the divine household shifted and changed for her. She assented to all the Lord's appointments. That is the faith which saves the soul, which agrees with the mind of God, even if it seem adverse to herself, which believes the revealed declarations of God whether they appear to be pleasant or terrible, and asserts to God's Word whether it be like a balm to its wound or like a sword to cut and slay. If the Word of God be true, O man, do not fight against it, but bow before it. It is not the way to a living faith in Jesus Christ, nor to obtain peace with God, to take up arms against anything which God declares. In yielding lies safety. Say "Truth, Lord," and you shall find salvation.

Note, that she not only assented to all that the Lord said, but *she worshiped Him in it.* "Truth," she said, "but yet You are my Lord." "You call me 'dog,' but You are my Lord for all that: You account me unworthy to receive Your bounties, but You are my Lord, and I still own You as such." She is of the mind of Job: "Shall we receive good at the hand of the Lord, and shall we not receive evil?" She is willing to take the evil and say, "Whether the Lord gives, or whether He refuses, blessed be His name; He is my Lord still." Oh, this is grand faith, which has thrown aside the disputatious spirit, and not only assents to the Lord's will, but worships Him in it. Let it be what it may, O Lord, even if the truth condemns me, yet still You are Lord, and I confess Your deity, confess Your excellence, own Your crown rights, and submit myself to You: do with me what You will."

And, you observe, when she said "Truth, Lord," *she did not go on to suggest that any alteration should be made for her.* "Lord," she said, "You have classed me among the dogs:" she does not say, "Put me among the children," but she only asks to be treated as a dog is. "The dogs eat the crumbs," says she. She does not want a purpose altered nor an ordinance changed, nor a decree removed: "Let it be as it is: if it be Your will, Lord, it is my will"; only she spies a gleam of hope, where, if she had not possessed faith, she would have seen only the blackness of despair. May we have such a faith as hers, and never enter into controversy with God.

Faith Argues Mightily

Now I come to an interesting part of our subject, namely, that FAITH ARGUES, though it does not dispute. "Truth, Lord," said she, "yet the dogs eat the crumbs." This woman's argument was correct, and strictly logical throughout. It was all argument based upon the Lord's own premises, and you know if you are reasoning with a man you cannot do better than take his own statements and argue upon them. She does not proceed to lay down new promises, or dispute the old ones by saying "I am no dog"; but she says, "Yes, I am a dog." She accepts that statement of the Lord, and uses it as a blessed *argumentum ad hominem*, such as was never excelled in this world. She took the words out of His own mouth, and vanquished Him with them, even as Jacob overcame the angel. There is so much force in the woman's argument, that I quite despair this morning of being able to set it all forth to you. I would, however, remark that the translators have greatly injured the text by putting in the word "yet," for there is no "yet" in the Greek: it is quite another word. Jesus said, "It is not meet to take the children's bread and cast it to the dogs." "No," said she, "it would not be meet to do this, because the dogs are provided for, for the dogs eat the crumbs that fall from their master's table. It would be very improper to give them the children's bread, because they have bread of their own. Truth, Lord, I admit it would be improper to give the dogs the children's bread, because they have already their share when they eat the crumbs which fall from the children's table. That is all they want, and all I desire. I do not ask You to give me the children's bread, I only ask for the dog's crumbs."

Let us see the force of her reasoning, which will appear in many ways. The first is this. *She argued with Christ from her hopeful position.* "I am a dog," said she, "but, Lord, You have come all the way to Sidon; here You are close on the borders of my country, and therefore I am not like a dog out in the street; I am a dog under the table." Mark tells us that she said, "The dogs under the table eat of the children's crumbs." She as good as says, "Lord, You see my position: I was a dog in the street, afar off from You, but now You have come and preached in our borders, and I have been privileged to listen to You. Others have been healed, and You are in this very house doing deeds of grace while I look on, and therefore, though I am a dog, I am a dog under the table; therefore, Lord, let me have the crumbs." Do you see, dear hearer? You admit that you are a sinner, and a great sinner, but you say, "Lord, I am a sinner that is permitted to hear the gospel, therefore bless it to me. I am a dog, but I am under the table, deal with me as such. When there is a sermon preached for the comfort of Your people, I am there to hear it: whenever the saints gather together, and the precious promises are discussed, and they rejoice therein, I am there, looking up, and wishing that I were among them, but still Lord, since You have had the grace to let me be a hearer of the gospel, will You reject me now that I desire to be a receiver of it? To what end and purpose have You brought me so near, or rather come so near to me, if after all You will reject me? Dog I am, but still I am a dog under the table. It is a favor to be privileged to be among the children, even if I may only be at their feet. I pray, good Lord, then, since now I am permitted to look up to You and ask this blessing, do not reject me." To me it seems that this was a strong point with the woman, and that she used it well.

Her next plea was her encouraging relationship. "Truth, Lord," she says, "I am a dog, but the dogs eat the crumbs which fall from *their master's* table." See the stress laid there by Matthew: "From their master's table." "I cannot say that You are my Father, I cannot look up and claim the privilege of a child, but You are my Master, masters feed their dogs;

they give at least the crumbs to those dogs which own them as their lord." The plea is very like that suggested to the mind of the poor returning prodigal. He thought to say to his father, "Make me as one of your hired servants": only his faith was far weaker than hers. "Lord, if I do not stand in relation to You as a child, yet I am Your creature; You have made me, and I look unto You and beseech You not to let me perish: if I have no other hold upon You I have at least this, that I ought to have served You, and therefore I am Your servant though I am a runaway. I do belong to You at least under the covenant of works if I do not under the covenant of grace, and oh, since I am Your servant, do not utterly reject me. You have some property in me by creation, at any rate; oh, look upon me, and bless me. The dogs eat what falls from their master's table, let me do the same." She spies out a dog's relation to its master, and makes the most of it with blessed ingenuity, which we shall do well to imitate.

Notice next, she pleads *her association with the children.* Here I must tell you that it is a pity that it was not, I suppose, possible for our translators to bring clearly out what is after all the pith of the passage. She was pleading for her *little* daughter; and our Lord said to her, "It is not meet to take the children's bread and cast it to the *little* dogs." The word is a diminutive, and the woman pitched upon it. The word "dogs" could not have served her turn one half as well as that of "little dogs," but she said, "Truth, Lord, yet the little dogs eat of the crumbs." In the East, as a rule, a dog is not allowed indoors; in fact, dogs are there looked upon as foul creatures, and roam about uncared for and half wild. Christianity has raised the dog, and made him man's companion, as it will raise all the brute creation, until the outrages of vivisection, and the cruelties of the vulgar, will be things unheard of except as horrors of a past barbarous age. In the East a dog is far down in the scale of life, a street wanderer, prowling for scanty food, and in temper little better than a reformed wolf. So the adult Easterns do not associate with dogs, having a prejudice against them, but children are not so foolish, and consequently the eastern children associate with the little dogs. The father will not have the dog near him, but his child knows no such folly, and seeks out a little dog to join him in his sports; thus the little dog comes to be under the table, tolerated in the house for the child's sake. The woman appears to me to argue thus—"You have called me and my daughter whelps, little dogs, but then the little dogs are under the children's table; they associate with the children, even as I have been with Your disciples today. If I am not one of them, I have been associating with them, and would be glad to be among them." How heartily do I wish that some poor soul would catch at this and say, "Lord, I cannot claim to be one of Your children, but I love to sit among them, for I am never happier than when I am with them. Sometimes they trouble and distress me, as little children pinch and hurt their little dogs, but oftentimes they caress me, and speak kindly and comfortably to me, and pray for me, and desire my salvation; so Lord, if I am not a child, yet You called me a little dog; so I am, but give me a little dog's treatment, give me a crumb of mercy which I seek."

Her argument goes further, for *the little dog eats the crumbs of the children's bread with the child's full consent*. When a child has its little dog to play with while he is eating, what does the child do? Why, of course, it gives a little bit to the dog every now and again, and the doggie himself takes great liberties and helps himself as much as he dares. When a little dog is with the children at meal time it is sure to get a crumb from one or other of its playmates; and none will object to its eating what it can get. So the woman seems to say, "Lord, there are the children, Your disciples; they do not treat me very well; little children do not treat little dogs always so kindly as they might; but still, Lord, they are quite willing that I should have the blessing I am seeking. They have a full portion in You; they have Your presence: they have Your word: they sit at Your feet; they have obtained all sorts of spiritual blessings: I am sure they cannot grudge me so much less a boon; they are willing that I should have the devil cast out of my daughter, for that blessing compared with what they have is but a crumb, and they are content that I should have it. So Lord, I answer Your argument. You say it is not meet until the children are filled to give bread to dogs, but, Lord, the children are filled and are quite willing to let me have my portion, they consent to allow me the crumbs; will You not give them to me?

I think there was another point of force in her plea: it was this, *the abundance of the provision*. She had a great faith in Christ, and believed big things of Him, and therefore she said, "Lord, there is no great strength in Your argument if You do intend to prove that I ought not to have the bread for fear there should not be enough for the children, for You have so much that even while the children are being fed the dogs may get the crumbs, and there will be enough for the children still." Where it is a poor man's table, and he cannot afford to lose a crumb, dogs should not be allowed; but when it is a king's table where bread is of small account, and the children are sitting and feeding to the full, the little dogs may be permitted to feed under the table for the mere droppings, not the bread the master *casts* down, but the crumbs which *fall* by accident are so many that there is enough for the dogs without the children being deprived of a mouthful. "No, Lord," said she, "I would not have You take away the bread from Your own children, God forbid that such a deed should be done for me but there is enough for Your children in Your overflowing love and mercy, and still enough for me, for all I ask is but a crumb compared with what You are daily bestowing upon others."

Now, here is the last point in which her argument had force. *She looked at things from Christ's point of view*. "If, great Lord," said she, "You look at me as a dog, then behold I humbly take You at Your word, and plead that if I be a dog to You then the cure I ask for my daughter is but a crumb for Your great power and goodness to bestow on me." She used a diminutive word too, and said, "A little crumb." The little dogs eat of the little crumbs which fall from the children's table. What bold faith this was! She valued the mercy she sought beyond all price; she thought it worth ten thousand worlds to her, but yet to the Son of God she knew it to be a mere crumb, so rich is He in power to heal and so full of goodness and blessing. If a man give a crumb to a dog He has a little the less, but if Jesus gives mercy to the greatest of sinners He has none the less, He is just as rich in condescension and mercy and power to forgive as He was before. The woman's argument was most potent. She was as wise as she was earnest, and best of all, she believed most marvelously.

I shall close this outline of the argument by saying that at bottom the woman was, in reality, arguing according to the eternal purpose of God; for what was the Lord's grand design in giving the bread to the children, or, in other words, sending a divine revelation to Israel? Why, it always was His purpose that through the children the dogs should get the bread; that through Israel the gospel should be handed to the Gentiles. It had always been His plan to bless His own heritage that His way might be known upon earth, His saving health among all nations; and this woman somehow or other, by a divine instinct, fell into the divine method. Though she had not spied out the secret, or at least it is not told us that she did so in so many words, yet there was the innate force of her argument. In other words, it ran thus—"It is through the children that the dogs have to be fed: Lord, I do not ask You to cease giving the children their bread; nor do I even ask You to hurry on the children's meal; let them be fed first, but even while they are eating let me have the crumbs which drop from their well-filled hands, and I will be content." There is a brave argument for you, poor coming sinner. I leave it in your hands, and pray the Spirit of God to help you to use it, and if you can turn it to good account you shall prevail with the Lord this day.

Faith Wins Her Suit

Our last and closing head is this: FAITH WINS HER SUIT. This woman's faith first *won a commendation for itself.* Jesus said, "O, woman, great is thy faith." She had not heard of the prophecies concerning Jesus; she was not bred and born and educated in a way in which she was likely to become a believer, and yet did become a believer of the first class. It was marvelous that it should be so, but grace delights in doing wonders. She had not seen the Lord before in her life, she was not like those who had associated with Him for many months: and yet, with but one view of Him, she gained this great faith. It was astonishing, but the grace of God is always astonishing. Perhaps she had never seen a miracle: all that her faith had to rest upon was that she had heard in her own country that the Messiah of the Jews was come, and she believed that the Man of Nazareth was He, and on this she relied. O brethren, with all our advantages, with the opportunities that we have of knowing the whole life of Christ and understanding the doctrines of the gospel as they are revealed to us in the New Testament, with many years of observation and experience, our faith ought to be much stronger than it is. Does not this poor woman shame us when we see her with her slender opportunities nevertheless so strong in faith, so that Jesus Himself commending her says, "O woman, great is thy faith."

But her faith prevailed further, that it *won a commendation for the mode of its action*, for, according to Mark, Jesus said, "Go thy way; *for this saying* the devil is gone out of thy daughter"; as if He rewarded the saying as well as the faith which suggested it. He was so delighted with the wise, and prudent, and humble yet courageous manner in which she turned His words against Himself, that He said, "For this saying the devil is gone out of thy daughter." The Lord who commends faith afterward commends the fruits and acts of faith. The tree consecrates the fruit. No man's actions can be acceptable with God until he himself is accepted, but the woman having been accepted on her faith, the results of her faith were agreeable to the heart of Jesus.

The woman also *gained her desire*: "The devil is come out of thy daughter," and he was gone at once. She had only to go home and find her daughter on the bed taking a quiet rest, which she had not done since the demon had possessed her. Our Lord, when He gave her the desire of her heart gave it in a grand manner, He gave her a sort of *carte blanche*, and said, "Be it unto thee even as thou wilt." I do not know that any other person ever had such a word said to him as this woman, "Be it unto thee even as thou wilt." It was as if the Lord of glory surrendered at discretion to the conquering arms of a woman's faith. The Lord grant to you and me in all times of our struggling to be able thus by faith still to conquer, and we cannot imagine how great will be the spoil which we shall divide when the Lord shall say, "Be it unto thee even as thou wilt."

The close of all is this: this woman is a lesson to all outsiders, to you who think yourselves beyond the pale of hope, to you who were not brought up to attend the house of God, who perhaps have been negligent of all religion for almost all your lifetime. This poor woman is a Sidonian; she comes of a race that had been condemned to die many centuries before, one of the accursed seed of Canaan, and yet for all that she became great in the kingdom of heaven because she believed, and there is no reason why those who are reckoned to be quite outside the church of God should not be in the very center of it, and be the most burning and shining lights of the whole. O you poor outcasts and far off ones, take heart and comfort, and come to Jesus Christ and trust yourselves in His hands.

This woman is next of all an example to those who think they have been repulsed in their endeavors after salvation. Have you been praying, and have you not succeeded? Have you sought the Lord, and do you seem to be more unhappy than ever? Have you made attempts at reformation and amendment, and believed that you made them in the divine strength, and have they failed? Yet trust in Him whose blood has not lost its efficacy, whose promise has not lost its truth, and whose arm has not lost its power to save. Cling to the cross, sinner. If the earth sink beneath you, cling on; if storms should rage, and all the floods be out, and even God Himself seems to be against you, cling to the cross. There is your hope. You cannot perish there.

This is a lesson, next, to every intercessor. This woman was not pleading for herself, she was asking for another. Oh, when you plead for a fellow sinner do not do it in a cold-hearted manner; plead as for your own soul and your own life. That man will prevail with God as an intercessor who solemnly bears the matter upon his own heart and makes it his own, and with tears entreats an answer of peace.

Lastly, recollect that this mighty woman, this glorious woman, is a lesson to every mother, for she was pleading for her little daughter. Maternal instinct makes the weakest strong, and the most timid brave. Even among poor beasts and birds, how powerful is a mother's love. Why, the poor little robin which would be frightened at the approach of a footstep, will sit upon its nest when the intruder comes near when her little ones are in danger. A mother's love makes her heroic for her child; and so when you are pleading with God plead as a mother's love suggests to you, until the Lord shall say to you also, "O woman, great is your faith; the devil is gone out of thy daughter; be it unto thee even as thou wilt." I leave that last thought with parents as an encouragement to pray. The Lord stir you up to it, for Jesus' sake. Amen.

7

*Martha and Mary**

Now it came to pass, as they went, that he entered into a certain village: and a certain woman named Martha received him into her house. And she had a sister called Mary, which also sat at Jesus' feet, and heard his word. But Martha was cumbered about much serving, and came to him, and said, Lord, dost thou not care that my sister hath left me to serve alone? bid her therefore that she help me. And Jesus answered and said unto her, Martha, Martha, thou art careful and troubled about many things: but one thing is needful: and Mary hath chosen that good part, which shall not be taken away from her (Luke 10:38–42).

It is not an easy thing to maintain the balance of our spiritual life. No man can be spiritually healthy who does not meditate and commune; no man, on the other hand, is as he should be unless he is active and diligent in holy service. David sweetly sang, "He maketh me to lie down in green pastures"; there was the contemplative, "he leadeth me beside the still waters"; there was the active and progressive: the difficulty is to maintain the two, and to keep each in its relative proportion to the other. We must not be so active as to neglect communion, nor so contemplative as to become unpractical. In the chapter from which our text is taken, we have several lessons on this subject. The seventy disciples returned from their preaching tour flushed with the joy of success; and our Savior, to refine that joy, and prevent its degenerating into pride, bids them rather rejoice that their names were written in heaven. He conducted their contemplations to the glorious doctrine of election, that grateful thoughts might sober them after successful work. He bids them consider themselves as debtors to the grace which reveals unto babes the mysteries of God, for He would not allow their new position as workers to make them forget that they were the

* This sermon was taken from *The Metropolitan Tabernacle Pulpit* and was preached on Sunday morning, April 24, 1870.

chosen of God, and therefore debtors. Our wise Master next returns to the subject of service, and instructs them by the memorable parable of the good Samaritan and the wounded man; and then as if they might vainly imagine philanthropy, as it is the service of Christ, to be the only service of Christ, and to be the only thing worth living for, he brings in the two sisters of Bethany; the Holy Spirit meaning thereby to teach us that while we ought to abound in service, and to do good abundantly to our fellow men, yet we must not fail in worship, in spiritual reverence, in meek discipleship, and quiet contemplation. While we are practical, like the seventy; practical, like the Samaritans; practical, like Martha; we are also, like the Savior, to rejoice in spirit, and say, "Father, I thank You," and we are also, like Mary, to sit down in quietude and nourish our souls with divine truth.

This short narrative I suppose might be paraphrased something after this fashion, Martha and Mary were two most excellent sisters, both converted, both lovers of Jesus, both loved by Jesus, for we are expressly told that He loved Mary and Martha and Lazarus. They were both women of a choice spirit, our Savior's selection of their house as a frequent resort proved that they were an unusually gracious family. They are persons representative of different forms of excellence, and I think it altogether wrong to treat Martha as some have done, as if she had no love for good things, and was nothing better than a mere worldling. It was not so. Martha was a most estimable and earnest woman, a true believer, and an ardent follower of Jesus, whose joy it was to entertain Jesus at the house of which she was the mistress. When our Lord made His appearance on this occasion at Bethany, the first thought of Martha was, "Here is our most noble guest, we must prepare for Him a sumptuous entertainment." Perhaps she marked our Savior's weariness, or saw some traces of that exhaustion which made Him look so much older than He was, and she therefore set to work with the utmost diligence to prepare a festival for Him; she was careful about many things, and as she went on with her preparations, fresh matters occurred to ruffle her mind, and she became worried; and, being somewhat vexed that her sister took matters so coolly, she begged the Master to upbraid her. Now Mary had looked upon the occasion from another point of view. As soon as she saw Jesus come into the house she thought, "What a privilege have I now to listen eagerly to such a teacher, and to treasure up His precious words! He is the Son of God, I will worship, I will adore, and every word He utters shall be stored in my memory. She forgot needs both of the Master and His followers, for her faith saw the inner glory which dwelt within Him, and she was so overpowered with reverence, and so wrapped in devout wonder that she became oblivious of all outward things. She had no faults to find with Martha for being so busy, she did not even think of Martha, she was altogether taken up with her Lord and with those gracious words which He was speaking. She had no will either to censure or to praise or to think even of herself; everything was gone from her but her Lord and the word which He was uttering. See then, that Martha was serving Christ, and so was Mary; Martha meant to honor Christ, so did Mary; they both agreed in their design, they differed in their way of carrying it out, and while Martha's service is not censured (only her being cumbered comes under the censure), yet Mary is expressly commended, as having chosen the good part; and therefore we do Martha no injustice if we show wherein she came short, and wherein Mary excelled.

Our first observation will be this, *the Martha spirit is very prevalent in the church of God just now*; in the second place, *the Martha spirit very much injures true service*; and, in the third place, *the Mary spirit is the source of the noblest form of consecration.*

The Martha Spirit is Very Prevalent in the Church of God

THE MARTHA SPIRIT IS VERY PREVALENT IN THE CHURCH at this period—prevalent in some quarters to a mischievous degree, and among us all to a perilous extent. What do we intend by saying that the Martha spirit is prevalent just now? We mean first, that *there is a considerable tendency among Christian people, in serving Christ, to aim at making a fair show in the flesh.* Martha wanted to give our Lord a right worthy entertainment which should be a credit to her house and to her family, and herein she is commendable far above those slovens who think anything good enough for Christ. So also, among professing Christians, there is at this present a desire to give to the cause of Christ buildings notable for their architecture and beauty. We must have no more barns, our meeting houses must exhibit our improving taste; if possible, our chapels must be correctly Gothic or sternly classical in all their details, both without and within. As to the service, we must cultivate the musical and the tasteful. We are exhorted not to be barely decent, but to aim at the sublime and beautiful. Our public worship, it is thought, should be impressive if not imposing; care should be taken that the music should be chaste, the singing conformed to the best rules of the art, and the preaching eloquent and attractive. So everything in connection with Christian labor should be made to appear generous and noble; by all means the subscription lists must be kept up; each denomination must excel the other in the amount of its annual funds; for surely everything done for Christ ought to be done in the best possible style. Now in all this there is so much that is good, so much that is really intended to honor the Lord, that we see no room to censure: but yet show we unto you a more excellent way. These things you may do, but there are higher things which you must do, or suffer loss. Brethren, there is something better to be studied than the outward, for though this may be aimed at with a single eye to God's glory, and we judge no man, yet we fear the tendency is to imagine that mere externals are precious in the Master's sight. I know He counts it a very small matter whether your house be a cathedral or a barn, to the Savior it is small concern whether you have organs or whether you have not, whether you sing after the choicest rules of psalmody or no; He looks at your hearts, and if these ascend to Him He accepts the praise. As for those thousands of pounds annually contributed, He estimates them not by the weights of the merchant but after the balances of the sanctuary. Your love expressed in your gifts He values, but what are the mere silver and gold to Him? Funds, and encouraging accounts, and well-arranged machineries are well if they exist as the outgrowth of fervent love, but if they are the end-all, and the be-all, you miss the mark. Jesus would be better pleased with a grain of love than a heap of ostentatious service.

The Martha spirit shows itself *in the censuring of those persons who are careful about Christ's word*, who stand up for the doctrines of the gospel, who desire to maintain the ordinances as they were delivered unto them, and who are scrupulous and thoughtful, and careful concerning the truth as it is in Jesus. In newspapers, on platforms, and in common talk, you frequently hear earnest disciples of Jesus and consistent believers in His doctrines scrupulous and denounced as unpractical. Theological questions are scouted as mere impertinences. Go in for ragged schools, certainly; reclaim the Arabs of the street, by all manner of means; pass a compulsory education bill, certainly; soup kitchens, free dinners, all excellent; we can all join in these; but never mention creeds and doctrines. Why, man, you cannot be aware of the enlightenment of our times! What importance can now be attached to mere biblical dogmas and ordinances? Why contend as to whether baptism shall be performed upon a babe or upon a believer, whether it shall be by sprinkling or by immersion? What matters the law of Christ in such a case? These things would do for the schoolmen of the dark ages to fight about, but what can be the importance of such trifles in this highly enlightened nineteenth century? Yes, that is the exaggeration of Martha. Mary, treasuring up every word of Christ, Mary counting each syllable a pearl, is reckoned to be unpractical, if not altogether idle. What spirit, I fear, is growing in these times, and needs to be checked; for, after all there is truth and there is error, and charitable talk cannot alter the fact. To know and to love the gospel is no mean thing. Obedience to Jesus, and anxiety to learn His will so as to please Him in all things, are not secondary matters. Contemplation, worship, and growth in grace are not unimportant. I trust we shall not give way to the spirit which despises our Lord's teaching, for if we do, in prizing the fruit and despising the root we shall lose the fruit and the root too. In forgetting the great well-spring of holy activity, namely, personal piety, we shall miss the streams also. From the sincerity of faith and the fervor of love practical Christianity must arise; and if the food that faith and love feed upon be withdrawn, if sitting at the feet of

Jesus be regarded as of secondary consequence, then both strength and will to serve the Lord will decline. I dread much the spirit which would tamper with truth for the sake of united action, or for any object under heaven—the latitudinarian spirit, which sneers at creeds and dogmas. Truth is no trifle. Not so thought our fathers, when at the stake they gave themselves to death, or on the brown heather of Scotland fell beneath the swords of Claverhouse's dragoons for truths which nowadays men count unimportant, but which, being truths, were to them so vital that they would sooner die than suffer them to be dishonored. O for the same uncompromising love of truth! Would to God we could be both active and studious, and both learn with Mary and work with Martha!

The Martha spirit crops up *in our reckoning so many things necessary.* Martha believed that to make Christ an entertainment, there must be many things prepared; as to leaving one of those things out—it could not be. Our Lord would have been satisfied enough with the simplest fare, a piece of fish or of a honeycomb would well have contented Him; but no, according to Martha's judgment there must be this, and there must be that. So is it with many good people now. They have their idea of excellence, and if these cannot be realized they despair of doing anything acceptable for Christ. I believe an educated ministry to be desirable, but nonetheless do I deplore the spirit which considers it to be essential. In the presence of the fishermen of Galilee we dare not subscribe to the necessity which with some is beyond doubt. You must not, according to the talk of some, allow these earnest young people to set about preaching, and your converted colliers and fiddlers should be stopped at once. The Holy Spirit has in all ages worked by men of His own choosing, but some churches would not let Him if they could help it. Their pulpits are closed against the most holy and useful preachers, if they have not those many things with which the church nowadays cumbers her ministers and herself. Then, my brethren, to carry on a good work, it is thought needful to have a society and large funds. I also approve of the society and the funds, I only regret that they should be so viewed as prime necessaries that few will stir without them. The idea of sending out a missionary with a few pounds in hand as in the days of Carey, is set down in many quarters as absurd. How can you save souls without a committee? How can London be evangelized until you have raised at least a million of money? Can you hope to see men converted without an annual meeting in Exeter Hall? You must have a secretary—there is no moving an inch until one is elected; and know you not that without a committee you can do nothing? All these and a thousand things which time fails me to mention, are now deemed to be needful for the service of Jesus, until a true-hearted soul who could do much for his Lord, scarcely dares to move until he has put on Saul's armor of human patronage. O for apostolical simplicity, going everywhere preaching the Word, and consecrating the labor of every believer to soul winning. To bring us back to first principles, "one thing is needful," and if by sitting at Jesus' feet we can find that one thing, it will stand us in better stead than all the thousand things which custom now demands. To catch the Spirit of Christ, to be filled with Himself, this will equip us for godly labor as nothing else ever can. May all Christians yet come to put this one thing first and foremost, and count the power of deep piety to be the one essential qualification for holy work.

The censurable quality in the Martha spirit appears in *the satisfaction which many feel with mere activity*. To have done so much preaching, or so much Sunday school teaching, to have distributed so many tracts, to have made so many calls by our missionaries, all this seems to be looked at as end rather than means. If there be so much effort put forth, so much work done, is it not enough? Our reply is, it is not enough, it is nothing without the divine blessing. Brethren, where mere work is prized, and the inner life forgotten, prayer comes to be at a discount. The committee is attended, but the devotional meeting forsaken. The gathering together for supplication is counted little compared with the collecting of subscriptions. The opening prayer at public meetings is regarded as a very proper thing, but there are those who regard it as a mere formality, which might be very well laid aside, and, therefore, invariably come in after prayer is over. It will be an evil day for us when we trust in the willing and the running, and practically attempt to do without the Holy Spirit.

The lofty estimate of mere activity, for its own sake, throws the acceptance of our work into the shade. The Martha spirit says, if the work is done, is not that all? The Mary spirit asks whether Jesus is well pleased or no? All must be done in His name and by His Spirit, or nothing is done. Restless service, which sits not at His feet, is but clattering of a mill which turns without grinding corn; it is but an elaborate method of doing nothing. I do not want less activity—how earnestly do I press you to it almost every Sabbath day; but I do pray that we may feel that all our strength lies in God, and that we can only be strong as we are accepted of Christ, and only can be accepted in Christ as we wait upon Him, in prayer, trust Him, and live upon Him. You may compass sea and land to make your proselytes, but if you have not the Spirit of Christ you are none of His. You may rise up early and sit up late, and eat the bread of sorrows, but unless you trust in the Lord your God you shall not prosper. The joy of the Lord is your strength. They that wait on the Lord shall renew their strength. Without Christ you can do nothing. Has He not told you, "He that abideth in me, and I in him, the same bringeth forth much fruit"? Was it not written of old, "I am like a green fir tree: from me is thy fruit found"?

Once more, Martha's spirit is predominant in the church of God to a considerable extent now, in *the evident respect which is paid to the man-*

ifest, and the small regard which is given to the secret. All regenerated persons ought to be workers for God and with God, but let the working never swamp the believing, never let the servant be more prominent than the son; never, because you conduct a class, or are chief man at a village station, forget that you are a sinner saved by grace, and have need still to be looking to the Crucified, and finding all your life in Him. You lose your strength as a worker if you forget your dependence as a believer. To labor for Christ is a pleasant thing, but beware of doing it mechanically; and this you can prevent by diligently cultivating personal communion with Christ. My brother, it may be you will undertake so much service that your time will be occupied, and you will have no space for prayer and reading the Word. The half-hour in the morning for prayer will be cut short, and the time allotted for communion with God in the evening will be gradually entrenched upon by this engagement and the other occupation, and when this is the case I tremble for you. You are killing the steed by spurring it and denying it food; you are undermining your house by drawing out the stones from the foundation to pile them at the top. You are doing your soul serious mischief if you put the whole of your strength into that part of your life which is visible to men, and forget that portion of our life which is secret between you and your God. To gather up all in one, I fear there is a great deal among us of religious activity of a very inferior sort; it concerns itself with the external of service, it worries itself with merely human efforts, and it attempts in its own strength to achieve divine results. The real working which God will accept is that which goes hand in hand with a patient waiting upon Christ, with heart scorching, with supplication, with communion, with a childlike dependence upon Jesus, with a firm adhesion to His truth, with an intense love to His person and an abiding in Him at all seasons; may we have more of such things. Martha's spirit, though excellent in itself so far as it goes, must not overshadow Mary's quiet, deep-seated piety, or evil will come of it.

The Martha Spirit Injures True Service

Secondly, we observe that THE MARTHA SPIRIT INJURES TRUE SERVICE.

Service may be true, and yet somewhat marred upon the wheel. Give your attention not so much to what I say, as to the bearing of it upon yourselves. It may be that you will find, as we speak, that you have been verily guilty touching these things. The Martha spirit *brings the least welcome offering to Christ.* It is welcome, but it is the least welcome. Our Lord Jesus when on earth was more satisfied by conversing to a poor Samaritan woman than He would have been by the best meat and drink. In carrying on His spiritual work He had meat to eat that His disciples knew not of. Evermore His spiritual nature was predominant over His physical nature, and those persons who brought Him spiritual gifts brought Him the gifts which He preferred. Here then was Martha's dish of well-cooked meat, but there was Mary's gift of a humble obedient heart; here was Martha decking the table, but there was Mary submitting her judgment to the Lord, and looking up with wondering eyes as she heard His matchless speech. Mary was bringing to Jesus the better offering. With Martha, He would in His condescension be pleased, but in Mary He found satisfaction. Martha's service He accepted benevolently, but Mary's worship He accepted with complacency. Now, brethren and sisters, all that you can give to Christ in any shape or form will not be so dear to Him as the offering of your fervent love, the clinging of your humble faith, the reverence of your adoring souls. Do not, I pray you, neglect the spiritual for the stake of the external, or else you will be throwing away gold to gather to yourself iron, you will be pulling down the palaces of marble that you may build for yourselves hovels of clay.

Martha's spirit has this mischief about it also, that *it brings self too much to remembrance*. We would not severely judge Martha, but we conceive that in some measure she aimed at making the service a credit to herself as the mistress of the house; at any rate, self came up when she began to grow weary, and complained that she was left to serve alone. *We* also want our work to show well as *our* work; we like those who see it to commend it, and if none commend it we feel that we are hardly done by, and are left to work alone. Now, to the extent in which I think of myself in my service I spoil it. Self must sink, and Christ be all in all. John the Baptist's saying must be our motto, "He must increase, I must decrease"; for Jesus' shoe latchet we are not worthy to unloose. Too much work and too little fellowship will always bring self into prominence. Self must be prayed down, and fellowship with Jesus must keep it down.

Martha seemed to fancy *that what she was doing was needful for Christ*. She was cumbered about much serving, because she thought it necessary that there should be a noble entertainment for the Lord. We are all too apt to think that Jesus wants our work, and that He cannot do without us. The preacher inquires what would become of the church if he were removed! The deacon is suspicious that if he were taken away there would be a great gap left in the executive of the church; the teacher of a class feels that these children would never be converted, Christ would miss of the travail of his soul but for him. Ah, but a fly on St. Paul's Cathedral might as well imagine that all the traffic at his feet was regulated by his presence, and would cease should he remove. I love you to think that Christ will do much work by you, and to attach as much weight as you can to your responsibilities, but as to Jesus needing us—the thing is preposterous. Mary is much wiser when she feels, "He desires me to receive His words, and yield Him my love; I would gladly give Him meat, but He will see to that; He is the Master of all things, and can do without me or Martha. I need Him far more than He can need me." We spoil our service when we overestimate its importance, for this leads us into loftiness and pride. Martha, under the influence of this high temper, came to complain of her sister, and to complain of her Lord too, as if He were excusing her idleness. "Dost thou not care that my sister hath left me to serve alone?" How it spoils what we do for Christ when we go about it with a haughty spirit; when we feel "I can do this, and it is grand to do that; am not I somewhat better than others? Must not my Master think well of me?" The humble worker wins the day. God accepts the man who feels his nothingness, and out of the depths cries to Him; but the great ones He will put down from their seats, and send the rich ones empty away. Activity, if not balanced by devotion, tends to puff us up, and so to prevent acceptance with God.

Martha also fell into an *unbelieving vexation.* Her idea of what was necessary to be done was so great that she found she could not attain to it. There must be this side dish, and there must be that principal joint, there must be this meat and that wine, it must be cooked just so many minutes, this must be done to a turn, and so on, and so on, and so on, and so on; and now time flies, she fears yonder guest has been slighted; that servant is not back from the market; many things go wrong when you are most anxious to have them right, You good housewives, who may have had large parties to prepare for, know what these cares mean, I dare say; and something of the sort troubled Martha, so that she became fretful and unbelieving. She had a work to do beyond her strength as the thought, and her faith failed her, and her unbelief went petulantly to complain to her Lord. Have we never erred in the same way? We must have that Sunday school excellently conducted, that morning prayer meeting must be improved, that Bible class must be revived, our morning sermon must be a telling one, and so on! The preacher here speaks of himself, for he sometimes feels that there is too much responsibility laid upon his shoulders, and he is very apt in reviewing his great field of labor to grow desponding in spirit. But when the preacher confessed that he spoke of himself, he only did so because he represents his fellow workers, and you also grow faint and doubtful. Alas! in such a case, the enjoyment of service evaporates, the fretfulness which pines over details spoils the whole, and the worker becomes a mere drudge and scullion instead of an angel who does God's commandments, hearkening unto the voice of His Word. Instead of glowing and burning like seraphs, our chariot wheels are taken off by our anxiety, and we drag heavily. Faith it is that secures acceptance, but when unbelief comes in, the work falls flat to the ground.

At such times when the man or the church shall become subject to the Martha spirit, *the voluntary principle falls a little into disrepute.* I believe the voluntary principle is the worst thing in all the world to work where there is no grace, but where there is grace it is the one principle that

God accepts. Now, Martha would have Mary *made* to serve Christ. What right has she to be sitting down there? Whether she likes or not she must get up and wait like her sister. Martha's voluntary desire to do much, leads her to think that Mary, if she has not quite such a voluntary love for the work must be driven to it, must have a sharp word from Christ about it. So it is with us. We are so willing to contribute to the Lord's work that we wish we had ten thousand times as much to give. Our heart is warm within us, and we feel we would make no reserve; and then are grieved with others because they give so very little, we wish we could compel them to give. And so we would put their cankered money into the same treasury with the bright freewill offerings of the saints, as if the Lord would receive such beggarly pittances squeezed out by force in the same manner as He accepts the voluntary gifts of His people. It were wiser if we left those unwilling contributions to rust in the pockets of their owners, for in the long run I believe they do not help the cause, for only that which is given out of a generous spirit, and out of love to Christ, will come up accepted before him. Too readily do we get away from the free spirit when we get away from the right spirit. The fact is, the Martha spirit spoils all, because it gets us away from the inner soul of service, as I have said before, to the mere husks of service; we cease to do work as to the Lord, we labor too much for the service sake; the main thing in our minds is the service, and not the Master; we are cumbered, and He is forgotten.

Thus have I indicated as briefly as I could, some of the weaknesses of the Martha spirit.

The Mary Spirit

I have to show you that it is capable of producing the noblest form of consecration to Christ. Its noblest results will not come just yet. Martha's fruits ripen very quickly, Mary's take time. When Lazarus was dead, you will remember Martha ran to meet Christ, but Mary sat still in the house; Martha wanted her own time, Mary could take Christ's time. So after awhile, just before our Lord's death, we find that Mary did a grand action, she did what Martha never thought of doing, she brought forth a box of precious ointment and poured it on the Lord's head, and anointed Him with ointment. While she was sitting at Christ's feet, she was forming and filling the springs of action. You are not losing time while you are feeding the soul. While by contemplation you are getting purpose strengthened and motive purified, you are rightly using time. When the man becomes intense, when he gets within him principles vital, fervent, energetic, then when the season for work comes he will work with a power and a result which empty people can never attain however busy they may be. If the stream flows at once, as soon as ever there is a shower, it must be little better than a trickling rivulet; but if the current stream is dammed up, so that for awhile nothing pours down the river bed, you will in due time, when the waters have gathered strength, witness a torrent before which nothing can stand. Mary was filling up the fountain head, she was listening and learning, feeding, edifying, loving, and growing strong. The engine of her soul was getting its steam ready, and when all was right her action was prompt and forcible. Meanwhile, *the manner of her action was being refined.* Martha's actions were good, but, if I may use the word, they were commonplace, she must make a great feed for the Lord Jesus, just as for any earthly friend; the spiritual nature of Christ she had forgotten, she was providing nothing for it; but Mary's estimate of Christ was of a truer order; she looked at Him as a priest, she viewed Him as a prophet, she adored Him as a king, and she had heard Him speak about dying, and had listened to His testimony about suffering, and dimly guessing what it meant, she prepared the precious spikenard that ere the dying should come she might anoint Him. The woman's deed was full of meaning and of instruction; it was indeed an embodied poem; the odor that filled the house was the perfume of love and elevated thought. She became refined in her actions by the process of musing and learning. Those who think not, who meditate not, who commune not with Christ, will do commonplace things very well, but they will never rise to the majesty of a spiritual conception, or carry out a heart suggested work for Christ.

That sitting of Mary was also *creating originality of act*. I tried two Sundays ago to enforce upon you the duty of originality of service as the right thing, that as we wandered everyone his own way we should each serve God in his own way, according to our peculiar adaptation and circumstances. Now this blessed woman did so. Martha is in a hurry to be doing something—she does what any other admirer of Jesus would do, she prepares meat and a festival; but Mary does what but one or two besides herself would think of, she anoints Him, and is honored in the deed. She struck out a spark of light from herself as her own thought, and she cherished that spark until it became a flaming act. I would that in the church of God we had many sisters at Jesus' feet who at last would start up under an inspiration and say, "I have thought of something that will bring glory to God which the church has not heard of before, and this will I put in practice, that there may be a fresh gem in my Redeemer's crown."

This sitting at the Master's feet guaranteed *the real spirituality of what she did.* Did you notice when I read what the Master said concerning the pouring of the ointment upon Him, "She *hath kept* this for my burial"? He praised her for keeping it, as well as for giving it. I suppose that for months she had set apart that particular ointment, and held it in reserve. Much of the sweetest aroma of a holy work lies in its being thought over and brought out with deliberation. There are works to be done at once and straightway, but there are some other works to be weighed and considered.

What shall I do my Savior to praise? There is a cherished scheme, there is a plan, the details of which shall be prayed out, and every single part of it sculptured in the imagination and realized in the heart, and then the soul shall wait, delighting herself in prospect of the deed, until the dear purpose may be translated into fact. It is well to wait, expectantly saying, "Yes, the set time will come, I shall be able to do the deed, I shall not go down to my grave altogether without having been serviceable; it is not yet the time, it is not yet the appropriate season, and I am not quite ready for it myself, but I will add grace to grace and virtue to virtue, and I will add self-denial to self-denial, until I am fit to accomplish the one chosen work." So the Savior praised Mary that she had kept this; kept it until the fit moment came before His burial; and then, but not until then, she had poured out and revealed her love. Ay, it is not your thoughtless service, performed while your souls are half asleep, it is that which you do for Christ with eyes that overflow, with hearts that swell with emotion, it is this that Jesus accepts. May we have more of such service, as we shall have if we have more of sitting at His feet. Christ accepted her, He said she had chosen the good part which should not be taken from her; and if our work be spiritual, intense, fervent, thoughtful, if it spring out of fellowship, if it be the outgushing of deep principles, of inward beliefs, of solemn gratitudes, then our piety shall never be taken from us, it will be an enduring thing, and not like the mere activities of Martha, things that come and go.

I have thus wrought out my text. I shall utter but two or three words upon the general applications of it. I shall apply it to three or four things yet briefly. Brethren, I believe in our Nonconformity; I believe if ever England wanted Nonconformists it is now; but there is a tendency to make Nonconformity become a thing of externals, dealing with state and church and politics. The political relations of Nonconformists, I believe in their value, I would not have a man less earnest upon them, but I am always fearful lest we should forget that Nonconformity is nothing if it be not spiritual, and that the moment we, as Dissenters, become merely political or formal, it is all over with us. Our strength is at the Master's feet, and I am afraid for our Nonconformity if it lives elsewhere. I mark so much conformity to the world, so much laxity of rule, so much love of novel opinions, that I tremble. I would we could go back to Puritanism. We are getting too lax, there is too much worldliness and carnality among us. There is little fear of our being censured, even by the world, for being too particular, I am afraid we are too much like the world for the world to hate us. As I pray that Nonconformity may always prevail in England, so I earnestly pray that she may stand because she abides near to Christ, holds His truth, prizes His word, and lives upon Himself.

Now the like is true of *missions*. Apply the principle there. God bless missions; our prayer goes up for them as warmly as for our soul's salvation. When shall the utmost ends of the earth behold the salvation of our God! But the strength of missions must lie not so much in arrangements, in committees, in journeys, in men, as in waiting up the Christ of God. We shall not do any more with a hundred thousand pounds, than with a single thousand, unless we get more grace; we shall not have more souls won with fifty missionaries than with five, unless we get ten times the amount of power from the right hand of the Most High. The waking up in missions needs to begin in our prayer meetings, and in our churches; in our personal wrestlings with God for the conversion of the heathen must lie the main strength of the workers that go out to do the deed. Let us remember this, Mary shall yet pour the box of ointment upon the head of the Anointed, Martha cannot do it.

The same thing is true in *revivals.* Persons will talk about getting up a revival—of all things I do believe one of the most detestable of transactions. "If you want a revival of religion," it is said, "you must get Mr. So-and-so to preach"—with him I suppose is the residue of the Spirit. Oh, but if you want a revival, you must adopt the methods so long in vogue, and so well known as connected with such-and-such a revival! I suppose the Spirit of God is no more a free Spirit, then, as He used to be in the olden times; and whereas of old He breathed where He listed, you fancy your methods and plans can control Him. It is not so; it is not so in any degree. The way to get the revival is to begin at the Master's feet; you must go there with Mary and afterward you may work with Martha. When every Christian's heart is set right by feeding on Christ's word and drinking in Christ's Spirit, then will the revival come. When we had the long drought, some farmers watered their grass, but found it did but very little good. An Irish gentleman remarked in my hearing that he had noticed that when it rained there were clouds about, and so all the air was in right order for the descent of rain. We have noticed thc same, and it so happens that the clouds and general constitution of the atmosphere have much to do with the value of moisture for the herbs. It is no good watering them in the sun, the circumstances do not benefit them. So with revivals. Certain things done under certain circumstances become abundantly useful, but if you have not similar circumstances, you may use the same machinery, but mischief instead of good will follow. Begin yourself with the Master, and then go outward to His service, but plans of action must be secondary.

So too, lastly, if you *want to serve God*, as I trust you do, I charge you first be careful of your own souls; do not begin with learning how to preach, or how to teach, or how to do this and that; dear friend, get the strength within your own soul, and then even if you do not know how to use it scientifically, yet you will do much. The first thing is, get the heart warmed, stir up your manhood, brace up all your faculties, get the Christ within you, ask the everlasting God to come upon you, get Him to inspire you, and then if your methods should not be according to the methods of others it will not matter, or if they should, neither will it be of consequence, having the power you will accomplish the results. But if you go about to perform the work before you have the strength from on high, you shall utterly fail. Better things we hope of you. God send them. Amen,

8

*Cured at Last!**

And a woman having an issue of blood twelve years, which had spent all her living upon physicians, neither could be healed of any, came behind him, and touched the border of his garment: and immediately her issue of blood stanched (Luke 8:43–44).

Though I take Luke's statement as a text, I shall constantly refer to the version of the same story which we find in Mark 5:25–29. Here we have one of the Lord's hidden ones: a case not to be publicly described because of its secret sorrow. We have here a woman of few words and much shamefacedness. Her malady subjected her to grievous penalties according to the ceremonial law. There is a terrible chapter in the Book of Leviticus concerning such a case as hers. She was unclean; everything that she sat upon, and all who touched it, shared in the defilement. So that, in addition to her continual weakness, she was made to feel herself an outcast, under the ban of the law. This created, no doubt, great loneliness of spirit, and made her wish to hide herself out of sight. In the narrative before us she said not a word until the Savior drew it out of her, for her own lasting good. She acted very practically and promptly, but she was a silent seeker: she would have preferred to have remained in obscurity, if so it could have been. Some here may belong to the great company of the timid and trembling ones. If courage before others is needed to secure salvation, matters will go hard with them, for they shrink from notice, and are ready to die of shame because of their secret grief. Cowper's hymn describes their inward feelings, when it says of the woman—

Conceal'd amid the gathering throng
　She would have shunn'd thy view,
And if her faith was firm and strong,
　Had strong misgivings too.

* This sermon was taken from *The Metropolitan Tabernacle Pulpit* and was preached on Sunday morning, April 8, 1888.

Such plants grow in the shade, and shrink from the light of the sun. The nature of their sorrows forces them into solitary self-communion. Oh, that the Lord may heal such at this hour!

The immediate cure of this woman is the more remarkable because it was a wayside miracle. The Savior was on the road to restore the daughter of Jairus; this woman's healing was an extra of grace, a sort of over-splash of the great fountain of mercy. The cup of our Lord's power was full—full to the brim—and he was bearing it to the house of the ruler of the synagogue; this poor creature did but receive a drop which He spilt on the way. *We* do well if, when going upon some errand of love, we concentrate all our energy upon it, and do it well in the end: but the Savior could not only perform one great marvel, but He could work another as a sort of by-play incidentally—I had almost said, accidentally, on the road. The episodes of the Lord Jesus are as beautiful as the main run of His life's poem. Oh, that this day, while my sermon may seem meant for one, and distinctly directed to His salvation, it may also, by the power of Jesus, save another not so clearly pointed at! While the word is aimed at one particular character, may the Lord cause the very wind of the gospel shot to overcome another: or, to change the figure for a better one, while we spread the table for some bidden guest, may another hungry soul have grace given Him to take His place at the banquet of grace! May those who hide away, and whom, therefore, we are not likely to discover, come forth to Jesus, and touch Him, and live!

Let us at once speak of this much-afflicted woman, for she is a typical character. While we describe *her* conduct and *her* cure, I trust she may serve as a looking-glass in which many tremblers may see themselves. We shall carefully note *what she had done*, and then *what came of it*. This will lead us on to see *what she did at last*, and *what we also should do*. May the Holy Spirit make this a very practical discourse by causing you to follow her until you gain the blessing as she did! The preacher is very weak; and may the Lord, for this very reason, work by him to your salvation.

What She Had Done

Consider, therefore, concerning this woman, WHAT SHE HAD DONE. She had been literally dying for twelve years. What had she been doing? Had she resigned herself to her fate, or treated her malady as a small matter? Far from it. Her conduct is highly instructive.

First, *she had resolved not to die if a cure could be had*. She was evidently a woman of great determination and hopefulness. She knew that this disease of hers would cause her life to ebb away, and bring her to the grave; but she said within herself, "I will have a struggle for it. If there is a possibility of removing this plague it shall be removed, let it cost me what it may of pain or payment." Oh, what a blessing it would be if unsaved ones here would say each one for himself, "I am a lost soul; but if a lost soul can be saved, I will be saved. I am guilty; but if guilt can be washed away, mine shall be washed away. I have a hard heart, and I know it; but if a heart of stone can be turned into a heart of flesh, I long to have it so, and I will never rest until this gracious work is wrought in me!" Alas, it is not so with many! Indifference is the rule; indifference about their immortal souls! Many are sick with dire spiritual disease, but they make no resolve to have it cured; they trifle with sin, and death, and heaven, and hell.

Insensibility has seized upon many, and a proud conceit: they are full of sin, and yet they talk of self-righteousness. They are weak, and can do nothing; yet they boast of their ability. They are not conscious of their true condition, and hence they have no mind to seek a cure. How should they desire healing when they do not believe that they are diseased? How sad that beneath the ruddy cheek of morality there should lurk the fatal consumption of enmity to God! How horrible to be fair without and leprous within! Are there not many who can talk freely about religion, and seem as if they were right with God, and yet in the secret of their hearts they are the victims of an insincerity, and a want of truth, which fatally undermine the life of their profession. They are not what they seem to be: a secret sin drains away the life-blood of their religion. May the Holy Spirit show every unregenerate person the fatal nature of his soul's disease; for this, I trust, would lead to the making of a firm resolve to find salvation, if salvation is to be had.

No doubt some are held back from such action by the freezing power of despair. They have reached the conclusion that there is no hope for them. The promises of the gospel they regard as the voice of God to others, but as having no cheering word for them. One might suppose that they had searched the book of life, and had made sure that their names were not written there; they act as if their death warrant had been signed. They cannot believe in the possibility of their becoming partakers of everlasting life. They are under a destroying delusion, which leads them to abandon hope. None are more presumptuous than the despairing. When men have no hope, they soon have no fear. Is not this a dreadful thing? May the Lord save you from such a condition! Despair of God's mercy is an unreasonable thing: if you think you have grounds for it, the lying spirit must have suggested them to you. Holy Scripture contains no justification for hopelessness. No mortal has a just pretense to perish in despair. Neither the nature of God, nor the gospel of God, nor the Christ of God, warrant despair. Multitudes of texts encourage hope; but no one Scripture, rightly understood, permits a doubt of the mercy of God. "All manner of sin and blasphemy shall be forgiven unto men." Jesus, the great Healer, is never baffled by any disease of human nature: He can cast out a legion of devils, and raise the dead. Oh that I could whisper hope into the dull ear of yonder mourner! Oh that I could drop a rousing thought into the sullen heart of the self-condemned! How glad should I be! My poor desponding friend, I would fain see your chains snapped, your fetters broken off! Oh that the Spirit of God would cause you, like this woman, to resolve that if there be healing for your soul you will have it!

Alas! many have never come to this gracious resolution, because they cherish a vain hope, and are misled by an idle dream. They fancy that salvation will come to them without their seeking it. Certainly, they have no right to expect such a thing. It is true that our Lord is found of them that sought Him not; but that is an act of His own sovereignty, and is not a rule for our procedure. The plain directions of the gospel are, "Seek ye the Lord while He may be found; call ye upon him while he is near." How dare they set these gracious words aside? They fancy that they may wake up, one of these fine days, and find themselves saved. Alas! it may more likely happen to them, as to the rich man in the parable, "In hell he lift up his eyes, being in torments." God grant that none of you may trifle your souls into such misery! Some fancy that in the article of death, they may cry, "God be merciful to me a sinner," and so may leap into salvation. It seems to them a very slight business to be reconciled to God. They imagine that they can be converted just when they will, and so they put it off from day to day, as if it were of no more consequence than going to shop to buy a coat or a gown. Believe me, the Word of God does not set forth the matter in this way. It tells us that even the righteous scarcely are saved, and it rouses us to strive to enter in at the strait gate. God save you from every false confidence which would prevent your being in earnest about the healing of your souls. Spiritually, your case is as desperate as that of the poor woman now before us. May the Lord sweetly constrain you to feel that you must be healed, and that you cannot afford to put off the blessed day! If beneath the firmament of heaven there is healing for a sin-sick soul, seek it until you find it. When the Lord brings you to this resolve by His good Spirit, you will not be far from the kingdom of heaven.

Let us next note, that *this woman having made her resolve, adopted the likeliest means she could think of*. Physicians are men set apart on purpose to deal with human maladies, therefore she went to the physicians. What better could she do? Though she failed, yet she did what seemed most likely to succeed. Now, when a soul is resolved to find salvation, it is most fit and proper that it should use every likely means for the finding of salvation. Oh, that they were wise enough to hear the gospel, and to come at once to Jesus; but often they make grave mistakes. This woman went to gentlemen who were supposed to understand the science of medicine. Was it not natural that she should look for help to their superior wisdom? She cannot be blamed for looking to the men of light and leading. Many, in these days, do the same thing. They hear of the new discoveries of professedly cultured men, and hear their talk about the littleness of sin, and the larger hope, and the non-necessity of the new birth. Poor deceived creatures! They find in the long run that nothing comes of it; for the wisdom of man is nothing but pretentious folly. The world by wisdom knows neither God nor His salvation. Many there are who know all the less of saving truth because they know so much of what human fancy has devised, and human search discovered. We cannot blame the woman that, being a simple soul, and anxious for healing, she went to those first who were thought to know most. Let us not, with Christ so near, go roundabout as she did, but let us touch our Lord at once.

No doubt the sufferer also tried men who had diplomas, or were otherwise authorized to act as physicians. How can you blame her for going to those who were in the succession, and had the official stamp? Many sin-sick souls nowadays are, at first, very hopeful that the ordained clergy can benefit them by their duly performed services and duly administered sacraments. At least, good men, eminent in the church, may be looked to for aid; surely these know how to deal with seals! Alas! it is vain to look to men at all, and foolish to depend on official dignity, or special repute. Some teachers do not know much about their own souls, and therefore know less about the souls of others. Vain is the help of man, be the man who he may. Whatever his popularity, learning, or eloquence, if you seek to him for his prayers, or his teachings, as able to save you, you will certainly seek in vain; as this poor woman did. She is not to be blamed, but to be commended, that she did what seemed best to her, according to her light; but you are warned; go not, therefore, to men.

No doubt she met with some who boasted that they could heal her complaint at once. They began by saying, "You have tried So-and-so, but he is a mere quack; mine is a scientific remedy. You have used a medicine which I could have told you would be worthless; but I have the secret. Put yourself absolutely into my hands, and the thing is done. I have healed many that have been given up by all the faculty. Follow my orders, and you will be restored." Sick persons are so eager to recover that they readily take the bait which is offered them by brazen impudence. An oily tongue and a bland manner, backed with unblushing assurance, are sure to win their way with one who is anxious to gain that which is offered. Ah, me! "All is not gold that glitters"; and all the professions which are made of helping sin-sick souls are not true professions. Many pretenders to new revelations are abroad, but they are physicians of no value. There is no balm in Gilead; there is no physician there: if there had been, the hurt of the daughter of my people had long ago been healed. There is no medicine beneath the sky that can stay the palpitations of a heart which dreads the judgment to come. No earthly surgery can take away the load of sin from the conscience. No hand of priest or presbyter, prophet or philosopher, can cleanse the leprosy of guilt. The finger of God is wanted here. There is one Heal-all, one divine *Catholicon*, and only one. Happy is he that has received this infallible balm from Jehovah Rophi—the Lord that heals. Yet we marvel not that when souls are pressed down with a sense of guilt, they try anything and everything which offers even a faint hope of relief. I could wish that all my hearers had an intense zeal to find salvation; for even if it led them into passing mistakes, yet, under God's blessing, they would find their way out of them, and end by glorifying the grace of our Lord Jesus Christ, which never fails.

This woman, in the next place, having resolved not to die if cure could be had, and having adopted the likeliest means, *persevered in the use of those means*. No doubt she tried many, and even opposite, remedies. One doctor said, "You had better go to the warm baths of the lake of Tiberias; such bathing will be comforting and helpful." She grew worse at the warm bath, and went to another physician, who said, "You were wrongly treated; you need bracing up in the cold baths of the Jordan." Thus she went from vanity to vanity, to find both of them useless. An eminent practitioner assured her that she needed an internal remedy, and he alone could give her an infallible receipt. This, however, was of no use to her; and she went to another, who said that an external application should be tried, such as Isaiah's lump of figs. What perseverance that woman must have had! I am not going to say anything about our doctors nowadays, no doubt they are the most learned and skillful that can be: but in earlier times surgery was murderous, and medicines were poisonous. Many of the prescriptions of those days are sickening, and yet ridiculous. I read yesterday a prescription of our Savior's time warranted to cure many diseases, which consisted of grasshopper's eggs. These were supposed to exercise a marvelous influence, but they are no longer in the list of medicines. The tooth of a fox was said to possess special powers; but I noticed that one of the chief drugs of all, the most expensive, but the surest in its action, was a nail from the finger of a man who had been hanged. It was important that he should have been hanged: another fingernail might have had no efficacy. Poor creatures were made to suffer most painfully by cruel medicines, which were far worse than the disease. As for surgical operations, if they had been designed to kill, they were certainly admirably arranged for their purpose. The wonder is that for twelve years poor human nature could stand out, not against the disease, but against the doctors. Brethren, the case is much the same spiritually. How many under their burden of sin go first to one, and then to another; practice this, and agonize after that, and pine for the other, perseveringly, and still without avail! Travel as fast as you may in a wrong direction, you will not reach the place you seek. Vain are all things save Jesus our Lord.

Have you been to Doctor Ceremony? He is, at this time, the fashionable doctor. Has he told you that you must attend to forms and rules? Has he prescribed you so many prayers, and so many services? Ah! many go to him, and they persevere in a round of religious observances, but these yield no lasting ease to the conscience. Have you tried Doctor Morality? He has a large practice, and is a fine old Jewish physician. "Be good in outward character," says he, "and it will work inwardly, and cleanse the heart." A great many persons are supposed to have been cured by him and by his assistant, Doctor Civility, who is nearly as clever as his master: but I have it on good evidence that neither of them apart, nor even the two together, could ever deal with an inward disease. Do what you may, your own doings will not stanch the wounds of a bleeding heart. Doctor Mortification has also a select practice; but men are not saved by denying themselves until they first deny their self-righteousness. Doctor Excitement has many patients, but his cures seldom outlive the set of sun. Doctor Feeling is much sought after by tender spirits; these try to feel sorrow and remorse; but, indeed, the way of cure does not lie in that quarter. Let everything be done that can be done apart from our blessed Lord Jesus Christ, and the sick soul will be nothing bettered. You may try human remedies for the space of a lifetime, but sin will remain in power, guilt will cling to the conscience, and the heart will abide as hard as ever.

But this woman not only thus tried the most likely means and persevered in the use of them, but *she also spent all her substance over it*. That was perhaps the chief thing in ancient surgery! This golden ointment which did good to the physician, whatever became of the patient. The most important point was to pay the doctor. This woman's living was wasting away as well as her life. She continued to pay, and to pay, and to pay; but she received no benefit from it all; say, rather, that she suffered more than she would have done had she kept her gold. Thus do men waste their thought, their care, their prayer, their agony over that which is as nothing: they spend their money for that which is not bread. At last she came to her last shekel. In the end there was an end to her means; but so long as the silver lasted, she lavished it out of the bag. What would not a man give to be saved? I never wonder that dying men give their estates to priests in the hope that they can save their souls. If gold could purchase pardon, who would withhold it? Health of body, if it could be purchased with gold, would be cheap at any price; but health of soul, holiness of character, acceptance with God, assurance of heaven—these would be cheap if we counted out worlds as poor men pay down their pence for bread. There are men so mean that they would not part with a pound for a place in Paradise; but if these once knew their true condition, they would alter their minds. The price of wisdom is above rubies. If we had mines of gold, we might profitably barter them for the salvation of our souls.

Beloved, you see where this woman was. She was in downright, desperate earnest to have her mortal malady healed, and so she spared neither her labor nor her living. In this we may wisely imitate her.

What Had Come of It

We have seen what the woman had done; now let us think of WHAT HAD COME OF IT. We are told that she had suffered many things of many physicians. That was her sole reward for trusting and spending: she had not been relieved, much less healed; but *she had suffered.* She had endured much additional suffering through seeking a cure. That is the case with you who have not come to Christ, but, being under a sense of sin, have sought relief apart from Him. All that you do apart from Jesus, in order to win salvation, will only cause you increased suffering. You have tried to save yourself by prayers; your prayers have turned your thoughts upon your sin and its punishment, and thus you have become more wretched than before. You have attended to ceremonies, and if you have used them sincerely, they have wrought in you a solemn sense of the holiness of God, and of your own distance from Him; and this, though very proper, has only increased your sorrow. You have been trying to feel good, and to do good that so you may be good; but the very effort has made you feel how far off you are from the goodness you so much desire. Your self-denial has excited cravings after evil, and your mortifications have given new life to your pride. Efforts after salvation made in your own strength act like the struggles of a drowning man, which sink the more surely. As the fruit of your desperate efforts, you have suffered all the more. In the end, I trust this may work for your good, but up until now it has served no healing purpose: you are now at death's door, and all your praying, weeping, church-going, chapel-going, and sacrament-taking, do not help you one bit.

There has been this peculiarly poignant pang about it all, that you are *nothing bettered.* Cheerily did you hope, but cruelly are you disappointed. You cried, "I have it this time," but the bubble vanished as you grasped it. The evil of your nature, when repressed in one place, broke out in another. You dealt with the symptoms of your disease, but you did not cut off the root of the mischief: it only showed itself in another form, but it never went away. You gave up one sin only to fall into another: you watched at the front entrance, and the thief stole in at the back door. Up until now, O soul, you have not come to Jesus, and after all your goings elsewhere, you are nothing bettered!

And now, perhaps, this morning you are saying, "What can I do? What shall I do?" I will tell you. You can do nothing except what this woman ultimately did, of which I will speak by-and-by. You are now brought to this extremity—that you are without strength, without merit, without power, and you must look out of yourself to another, who has strength and merit, and can save you. God grant that you may look to that glorious One before this service is over!

We read of this woman, that though she suffered much, she was nothing better, but *rather grew worse.* No better after twelve years of medicine? She went to the Egyptian doctor, and he promised her health in three months. She was worse. She tried the Syrian doctor: he was a man who had great knowledge of the occult sciences, and was not ashamed to practice enchantments. She was bitterly disappointed to find herself decidedly weaker. Then she heard of a Greek practitioner, who would cure her, heigh presto! in a trice. She paid her remaining money, but she still went backward. She bought disappointment very dearly. Friend, is this your condition? You are anxious to be right, and, therefore, you are earnest in every effort to save yourself; but still you are nothing bettered. You climb a treadmill, and are no higher after all your climbing. You drift down the river with one tide, and you float up again when it turns. Night after night you pull up in the same old creek that you started from. Oh, pitiful condition! Getting gray, too: becoming quite the old gentleman; and yet no nearer eternal life than when, as a lad, you used to attend the house of God, and wish to become a child of God. Nothing bettered? No; she grew worse? Fresh mischief had developed: other diseases fed upon her weakness; she was more emaciated, more lifeless than ever. Sad result of so much perseverance! And is not that the case with some of you who are in earnest, but are not enlightened? You are working, and growing poorer as you work. There is not about you so much as there used to be of good feeling, or sincere desire, or prayerfulness, or love for the Bible, or care to hear the gospel. You are becoming more careless, more dubious than you once were. You have lost much of you former sensitiveness. You are doing certain things now that would have startled you years ago, and you are leaving certain matters undone which once you would have thought essential. Evidently you are caught in the current, and are nearing the cataract. The Lord deliver you!

This is a sad, sad case! As a climax of it all, the heroine of our story had now *spent all that she had.* She could not go now to the Egyptian doctor, or to the Syrian doctor, or to the Hebrew doctor, or to the Roman doctor, or to the Greek doctor. No; now she must do without their flattering unction in the future. As for those famous medicines which raised her hopes, she can buy no more of such costly inventions. This was, perhaps, her bitterest grief: but let me whisper it in your ear—this was the best thing that had yet happened to her; and I am praying that it may happen to some of you. At the bottom of your purse I trust you will find wisdom. When we come to the end of self we come to the beginning of Christ. That last shekel binds us to the pretenders, but absolute bankruptcy sets us free to go to Him who heals diseases without money and without price. Glad enough am I when I meet with a man who is starved out of self-sufficiency. Welcome, brother! Now you are ready for Jesus. When all your own virtue has gone out of you, then shall you seek and find that virtue which goes out of Him.

What This Woman Did at Last

This brings to our notice, in the third place, WHAT THIS WOMAN DID AT LAST. Weaker and weaker had she become, and her purse had become lighter and lighter. She hears of Jesus of Nazareth, a man sent of God who is healing sick folk of all sorts. She hears attentively; she puts the stories together that she hears; she believes them; they have the likeness of truth about them. "Oh," says she, "there is yet another opportunity for me. I will get in the crowd, and if I can only touch the bit of blue which He wears as the border of His garment, I shall be made whole." Splendid faith! It was thought much of in her own day, and we may still more highly prize it now that faith has grown so rare.

Note well *she resolved to trust in Jesus in sheer despair of doing anything else.* My dear friend, I do not know where you are sitting this morning in this great congregation—I almost wish I did, that I might come up to you and say to you personally, "Try Jesus Christ, trust Him, and see whether He will not save you. Every other door is evidently shut; why not enter by Christ the door? There is no other life-buoy; lay hold on this! Say with our versifier—

> I can but perish if I go;
> I am resolved to try;
> For if I stay away, I know
> I must forever die.

Exercise the courage which is born of desperation. May God the Holy Spirit help you now to thrust forth your finger, and get into touch with Jesus! Say, "Yes, I freely accept Christ. By God's grace, I will have Him to be my only hope. I will have Him now." Be driven to Jesus by force of circumstances. Since there is no other port, O weather-beaten barque, make for this one! Wanderer, here is a refuge! Turn in hither, for there is no other shelter.

After all, *this was the simplest and easiest thing that she could do.* Touch Jesus. Put out your finger, and touch the hem of His garment. The prescriptions she had purchased were long; but this was short enough. The operations performed upon her had been intricate; but this was simplicity itself. The suffering she had endured had complicated her case; but this was as plain as a pikestaff. "Touch with your finger the hem of His garment: that is all." O my hearer, you have tried many things, great things, and hard things, and painful things: why not try this simple matter of faith? Believe in the Lord Jesus Christ, and you shall be saved. Trust Jesus to cleanse you, and He will do it. Put yourself into your Savior's hands once for all, and He will save you.

Not only was this the simplest and easiest thing for the poor afflicted one, but certainly *it was the freest and most gracious.* There was not a penny to pay. Nobody stood at the door of the consulting room to take her guinea; and the good physician did not even give a hint that He expected a reward. The gifts of Jesus are free as the air. He healed this believing woman in the open street, in the midst of the crowd. She had felt that if she could but get into the throng, she would, by hook or by crook, get near enough to reach the hem of His garment, and then she would be healed. It is so this morning, dear hearer. Come, and receive grace freely. Bring no good works, no good words, no good feelings, no good resolves, as the price of pardon; come with an empty hand, and touch the Lord by faith. The good things which you desire, Jesus will give you as the result of His cure; but they cannot be the cause or the price of it. Accept His mercy as the gift of His love! Come empty-handed, and receive! Come undeserving, and be favored! Only come into contact with Jesus, who is the fountain of life and health, and you shall be saved.

This was the quietest thing for her to do. She said nothing. She did not cry aloud like the blind men. She did not ask friends to look on, and see her make her venture. She kept her own counsel, and pushed into the press. In absolute silence, she took a stolen touch of the Lord's robe. O my hearer, you can be saved in silence. You have no need to speak to any person of your acquaintance, not even to mother or father. At this moment, while in the pew, believe and live. Nobody will know that you now are touching the Lord. In after days you will own your faith, but in the act itself you will be alone and unseen. Believe on Jesus. Trust yourself with Him. Have done with all other confidences, and say, "He is all my salvation." Take Jesus at once, if not with a hand's grasp, yet with a finger's touch. O you poor, timid, bashful creature, touch the Lord! Trust in His power to save. Do not let me tell you to do it in vain, but do it at once. May God's Spirit cause you to accept Jesus now!

This is *the only effectual thing.* Touch Jesus, and salvation is yours at once. Simple as faith is, it is never-failing. A touch of the fringe of the Savior's garment sufficed: in a moment she felt in her body that she was healed of that plague. "It is twelve years ago," she said to herself, "since I felt like a living woman. I have been sinking in a constant death all this while, but now I feel my strength come back to me." Blessed be the name of the great Healer! She was exceeding glad. Tremble she did, lest it should turn out to be too good to be true; but she was most surely healed. O my dear hearer, do trust my Lord, for He will surely do for you that which none other can achieve. Leave feeling and working, and try faith in Jesus. May the Holy Spirit lead you to do so at once!

Do as This Woman Did

And now, poor convicted sinner! here comes the driving home of the nail. DO AS THIS WOMAN DID. Ask nobody about it, but do it. She did not go to Peter, James, and John, and say, "Good sirs, advise me." She did not beg from them an introduction to Jesus, but she went of her own accord, and tried for herself the virtue of a touch. You have had advising enough; now come to real work. There is too much tendency to console ourselves by conversations with godly men: let us get away from them, and speak to their Master. Talks in the inquiry room, and chats with Christian neighbors, are all very well; but one touch of Jesus will be infinitely better. I do not blame you for seeking religious advice: this may be a half-way house to call at, but do not make it the terminus. Press on until, by personal faith, you have laid hold on Jesus. Do not tell anybody what you are about to do; wait until it is done. Another day you will be happy to tell the minister and God's people of what the Lord has done for you; but for the present, quietly believe in the Lamb of God which takes away the sin of the world.

Do not even ask yourself about it. If this poor woman had consulted with herself, she might never have ventured so near the holy One of God. So clearly shut out from society by the law of her people and her God, if she had given the matter a second thought, she might have abandoned the idea. Blessed was the impetuosity which thrust her into the crowd, and kept her head above the throng, and her face toward the Lord in the center of the press. She did not so much reason as dare. Do not ask yourself anything about it; but do it. Believe, and have done with it. Stop not to parley with your own unbelief, nor answer your rising doubts and fears; but at once, upon the instant, put out your finger, touch the hem of His garment, and see what will come of it. God help you to do so while I am speaking!

Yield to the sacred impulse which is just now operating upon you. Do not say, "Tomorrow may be more convenient." In this woman's case, there was the Lord before her; she longed to be healed at once, and so, come what may, into the crowd she plunged. She was so enfeebled, that one wonders how she managed to get near Him; but possibly the crowd took her off her feet and carried her onward, as often happens in a rush. However, there was her chance, and she seized it. There was the fringe of the Lord's mantle; out went her finger: it was all done. O my friend, you have an opportunity now, by God's great grace, for you are in His house of prayer. Jesus of Nazareth passes by at this moment. He who speaks to you is not trying to say pretty things, but He is pining to win your soul for Jesus. Oh, how I wish I could lead you to that saving touch! The Spirit of God can do it. May He now move you to cry—"I will believe in the appointed sacrifice, and trust my soul with Jesus"! Have you done so? You are saved. "He that believeth in him hath everlasting life."

"Oh, but I tremble so!" So did she whom Jesus healed. Her hand shook, but she touched Him all the same for that. I think I see her quivering finger. Poor emaciated woman, with pale and bloodless cheeks! What a taper finger was that which she held out, and how it quivered! However much the finger of your faith may tremble, if it does but touch the hem of the Lord's garment, virtue will flow from Him to you. The power is not in the finger which touches, but in the divine Savior who is touched. So long as there is a contact established between you and the almighty power of Jesus, His power will travel along your trembling finger, and bring healing to your heart. A telegraph wire may shake with the wind, and yet convey the electric current, and so may a trembling faith convey salvation from Jesus. A strong faith, which rests anywhere but in Jesus, is a delusion; but a weak faith, which rests alone on Jesus, brings sure salvation. Out with your finger! Dear soul, out with your finger! Do not go away until you have touched the Lord by a believing prayer or hope. Holy Spirit, do not suffer any to quit the Tabernacle until, by a believing desire, or trust, or confidence of some sort, they have established a contact between themselves and Jesus, and have felt the virtue enter them for their instant healing. O Lord, save this people! Why do you come, Sunday after Sunday, in such crowds? And why must I stand here and bleed my heart away in love to your souls? Is the sole result to be that I help you to spend an hour-and-a-half in a sort of religious amusement? What a waste it is of my labor, and of your time, unless some gracious work is done! O sirs, if you are not brought to Christ, my preaching will prove a curse to you! It appalls me to think that the preaching of the gospel will be a savor of death unto you unless it brings you life. Put not the day of grace from you. By the living God, I do implore you, trust the living Redeemer. As I shall meet you all, face-to-face, before the judgment seat of Christ, I do implore and beseech you, put out the finger of faith, and trust the Lord Jesus, who is so fully worthy to be trusted. The simple trust of your heart will stay the death which now works in you. Lord, give that trust, for Jesus' sake! Amen.

9

*The Importunate Widow**

And he spake a parable unto them to this end, that men ought always to pray, and not to faint; saying, There was in a city a judge, which feared not God, neither regarded man: and there was a widow in that city; and she came unto him, saying, Avenge me of mine adversary. And he would not for a while: but afterward he said within himself, Though I fear not God, nor regard man; yet because this widow troubleth me, I will avenge her, lest by her continual coming she weary me. And the Lord said, Hear what the unjust judge saith. And shall not God avenge his own elect, which cry day and night unto him, though he bear long with them? I tell you in that he will avenge them speedily (Luke 18:1–8).

Remember that our Lord did not only inculcate prayer with great earnestness, but He was Himself a brilliant example of it. It always gives force to a teacher's words when his hearers well know that he carries out his own instructions. Jesus was a prophet mighty both in deed and in word, and we read of Him, "Jesus began both to do and to teach." In the exercise of prayer, "cold mountains and the midnight air" witnessed that He was as great a doer as a teacher. When He exhorted His disciples to continue in prayer, and to "pray without ceasing," He only made them follow in His steps. If any one of all the members of the mystical body might have been supposed to need no prayer, it would certainly have been our Covenant Head, but if our Head abounded in supplication, much more ought we, the inferior members. He was never defiled with the sins which have debased and weakened us spiritually; He had no inbred lusts to struggle with. But if the perfectly pure drew near so often unto God, how much more incessant in supplication ought we to be! So mighty, so great, and yet so prayerful! O you weak ones of the flock, how

* This sermon was taken from *The Metropolitan Tabernacle Pulpit* and was preached on Sunday morning, February 21, 1869.

forcibly does the lesson come home to you! Imagine, therefore, the discourse of this morning is not preached to you by me, but comes fresh from the lips of One who was the great Master of secret prayer, the highest paragon and pattern of private supplication, and let every word have the force about it as coming from such a One.

Turn we at once to our text, and in it we shall notice, first, *the end and design of the parable*; secondly, we shall have some words to say upon *the two actors in it*, whose characters are intentionally so described as to give force to the reasoning; and then, thirdly, we shall dwell upon *the power which in the parable is represented as triumphant.*

Our Lord's Design in This Parable

First, then, consider OUR LORD'S DESIGN IN THIS PARABLE—"Men ought always to pray, and not to faint."

But can men pray always? There was a sect in the earlier days of Christianity who were foolish enough to read the passage literally, and to attempt praying without ceasing by continual repetition of prayers. They of course separated themselves from all worldly concerns, and in order to fulfill one duty of life neglected every other. Such madmen might well expect to reap the due reward of their follies. Happily there is no need in this age for us to reprobate such an error; there is far more necessity to cry out against those who, under the pretense of praying always, have no settled time for prayer at all, and so run to the opposite extreme. Our Lord meant by saying men ought always to pray, *that they ought to be always in the spirit of prayer*, always ready to pray. Like the old knights, always in warfare, not always on their steeds dashing forward with their lances in rest to unhorse an adversary, but always wearing their weapons where they could readily reach them, and always ready to encounter wounds or death for the sake of the cause which they championed. Those grim warriors often slept in their armor; so even when we sleep, we are still to be in the spirit of prayer, so that if perchance we wake in the night we may still be with God. Our soul, having received the divine centripetal influence which makes it seek its heavenly center, should be evermore naturally rising toward God Himself. Our heart is to be like those beacons and watch-towers which were prepared along the coast of England when the invasion of the Armada was hourly expected, not always blazing, but with the wood always dry, and the match always there, the whole pile being ready to blaze up at the appointed moment. Our souls should be in such a condition that ejaculatory prayer should be very frequent with us. No need to pause in business and leave the counter, and fall down upon the knees; the spirit should send up its silent, short, swift petitions to the throne of grace. When Nehemiah would ask a favor of the king, you will remember that he found an opportunity to do so through the king's asking him, "Why art thou sad?"

but before he made him an answer he says, "I prayed unto the King of heaven"; instinctively perceiving the occasion, he did not leap forward to embrace it, but he halted just a moment to ask that he might be enabled to embrace it wisely and fulfill his great design therein. So you and I should often feel, "I cannot do this until I have asked a blessing on it." However impulsively I may spring forward to gain an advantage, yet my spirit, under the influence of divine grace, should hesitate until it has said, "If thy Spirit go not with me, carry me not up hence." A Christian should carry the weapon of all-prayer like a drawn sword in his hand. We should never sheathe our supplications. Never may our hearts be like an unlimbered gun, with everything to be done to it before it can thunder on the foe, but it should be like a piece of cannon, loaded and primed, only requiring the fire that it may be discharged. The soul should be not always the exercise of prayer, but always in the energy of prayer; not always actually praying, but always intentionally praying.

Further, when our Lord says, men ought always to pray, He may also have meant that *the whole life of the Christian should be a life of devotion to God.*

> Prayer and praise with sins forgiven,
> Brings down to earth the bliss of heaven.

To praise God for mercies received both with our voices and with our actions, and then to pray to God for the mercies that we need, devoutly acknowledging that they come from Him, these two exercises in one form or other should make up the sum total of human life. Our life psalm should be composed of alternating verses of praying and of praising until we get into the next world, where the prayer may cease, and praise may swallow up the whole of our immortality. "But," says one, "we have our daily business to attend to." I know you have, but there is a way of making business a part of praise and prayer. You say, "Give us this day our daily bread," and that is a prayer as you utter it; you go off to your work, and as you toil, if you do so in a devout spirit, you are actively praying the same prayer by your lawful labor. You praise God for the mercies received in your morning hymn; and when you go into the duties of life, and there exhibit the graces which reflect honor upon God's name, you are continuing your praises in the best manner. Remember that with Christians to labor is to pray, and that there is much truth in the verse of Coleridge—

> He prayeth best who loveth best.

To desire my fellow creatures' good and to seek after it, to desire God's glory, and so to live as to promote it, is the truest of devotion. The devotion of the cloisters is by no means equal to that of the man who is engaged in the battle of life; the devotion of the nunnery and the monastery is at best the heroism of a soldier who shuns the battle; but the devotion of the man in business life, who turns all to the glory of God, is the courage of one who seeks the thickest of the fray, and there hears aloft the grand old standard of Jehovah-nissi. You need not be afraid that there is anything in any lawful calling that need make you desist from vital prayer; but, oh! if your calling is such that you cannot pray in it, you had better leave it. If it be a sinful calling, an unholy calling, of course, you cannot present that to God, but any of the ordinary avocations of life are such that if you cannot sanctify them, it is a want of sanctity in yourself, and the fault lies with you. Men ought *always* to pray. It means that when they are using the lapstone, or the chisel, when the hands are on the plow handles, or on the spade, when they are measuring out the goods, when they are dealing in stocks, whatever they are doing, they are to turn all these things into a part of the sacred pursuit of God's glory. Their common garments are to be vestments, their meals are to be sacraments, their ordinary actions are to be sacrifices, and they themselves a royal priesthood, a peculiar people zealous for good works.

A third meaning which I think our Lord intended to convey to us was this: men ought always to pray, that is, *they should persevere in prayer*. This is probably His first meaning. When we ask God for a mercy once, we are not to consider that now we are not further to trouble Him with it, but we are to come to Him again and again. If we have asked of Him seven times, we ought to continue until seventy times seven. In temporal mercies there may be a limit, and the Holy Spirit may bid us ask no more. Then must we say, the "Lord's will be done." If it be anything for our own personal advantage, we must let the Spirit of submission rule us, so that after having sought the Lord thrice, we shall be content with the promise, "My grace is sufficient for thee," and no longer ask that the thorn in the flesh should be removed. But in spiritual mercies, and especially in the united prayers of a church, there is no taking a denial. Here, if we would prevail, we must persist; we must continue incessantly and constantly, and know no pause to our prayer until we win the mercy to the fullest possible extent. "Men ought always to pray." Week by week, month by month, year by year; the conversion of that dear child is to be the father's main plea. The bringing in of that unconverted husband is to be upon the wife's heart night and day until she gets it; she is not to take even ten or twenty years of unsuccessful prayer as a reason why she should cease; she is to set God no times nor seasons, but so long as there is life in her and life in the dear object of her solicitude, she is to continue still to plead with the mighty God of Jacob. The pastor is not to seek a blessing on his people occasionally, and then in receiving a measure of it to desist from further intercession, but he is to continue vehemently without pause, without restraining his energies, to cry aloud and spare not until the windows of heaven be opened and a blessing be given too large for him to house. But, brethren, how many times we ask of God, and have not because we do not wait long enough at the door! We knock a time or two at the gate of mercy, and as no friendly messenger opens the door, we go our ways. Too many prayers are like boys' runaway knocks, given, and then the giver is away before the door can be opened. O for grace to stand foot to foot with the angel of God, and never, never, never relax our hold; feeling that the cause we plead is one in which we must be successful, for souls depend on it, the glory of God is connected with it, the state of our fellow men is in jeopardy. If we could have given up in prayer our own lives and the lives of those dearest to us, yet the souls of men we *cannot* give up, we must urge and plead again and again until we obtain the answer.

The humble suppliant cannot fail
To have his wants supplied,
Since he for sinners intercedes
Who once for sinners died.

I cannot leave this part of the subject without observing that our Lord would have us learn that *men should be more frequent in prayer*. Not only should they always have the spirit of prayer, and make their whole lives a prayer, and persevere in any one object which is dear to their souls, but there should be a greater frequency of prayer among all the saints. I gather that from the parable, "lest by her continual coming she weary me." Prayerfulness will scarcely be kept up long unless you set apart times and seasons for prayer. There are no times laid down in Scripture except by the example of holy men, for the Lord trusts much to the love of His people and to the spontaneous motions of the inner life. He does not say, "Pray at seven o'clock in the morning every day," or "pray at night at eight, or nine, or ten, or eleven" but says, "Pray without ceasing." Yet every Christian will find it exceedingly useful to have his regular times for retirement, and I doubt whether any eminent piety can be maintained without these seasons being very carefully and scrupulously observed. We read in the old traditions of James the apostle, that he prayed so much that his knees grew hard through his long kneeling: and it is recorded by Fox, that Latimer, during the time of his imprisonment was so much upon his knees that frequently the poor old man could not rise to his meals, and had to be lifted up by his servants. When he could no longer preach, and was immured within stone walls, his prayers went up to heaven for his country, and we in these times are receiving the blessing. Daniel prayed with his windows open daily and at regular intervals. "Seven times a day" says one, "will I praise You." David declared that at "Evening, and morning, and at noon," would he wait upon God. O that our intervals of prayer were not so distant one from the other; would God that on the pilgrimage of life the wells at which we drink were more frequent. In this way should we continue in prayer.

Our Lord means, to sum up the whole, that *believers should exercise a universality of supplication*—we ought to pray at all times. There are no canonical hours in the Christian's day or week. We should pray from cock-crowing to midnight, at such times as the Spirit moves us. We should pray in all estates, in our poverty and in our wealth, in our health and in our sickness, in the bright days of festival and in the dark nights of lamentation. We should pray at the birth and pray at the funeral, we should pray when our soul is glad within us by reason of abundant mercy, and we should pray when our soul draws nigh unto the gates of death by reason of heaviness. We should pray in all transactions, whether secular or religious. Prayer should sanctify every thing. The Word of God and prayer should come in over and above the common things of daily life. Pray over a bargain, pray over going into the shop and coming out again. Remember in the days of Joshua how the Gibeonites deceived Israel because Israel inquired not of the Lord, and be not you deceived by a specious temptation, as you may well be if you do not daily come to the Lord, and say, "Guide me: make straight a plain path for my feet, and lead me in the way everlasting." You shall never err by praying too much, you shall never make a mistake by asking God's guidance too often; but you shall find this to be the gracious illumination of your eyes, if in the turning of the road where two paths meet which seem to be equally right, you shall stay a moment and cry unto God, "Guide me, O thou great Jehovah." "Men ought always to pray." I have enlarged upon it from this pulpit, go you and expound it in your daily lives.

The Two Actors

In enforcing this precept, our Lord gives us a parable in which there are TWO ACTORS, the characteristics of the two actors being such as to add strength to His precept.

In the first verse of the parable there is *a judge*. Now, herein is the great advantage to us in prayer. Brethren, if this poor woman prevailed with a judge whose office is stern, unbending, untender, how much more ought you and I to be instant in prayer and hopeful of success when we have to supplicate a Father! Far other is a father than a judge. The judge must necessarily be impartial, stern, but the father is necessarily partial to his child, compassionate and tender to his own offspring. Does she prevail over a judge; and shall not we prevail with our Father who is in heaven? And does she continue in her desperate need to weary him until she wins what she desires; and shall not we continue in the agony of our desires until we get from our heavenly Father whatsoever His Word has promised?

In addition to being a judge, he was *devoid of all good character*. In both branches he failed. He "feared not God." Conscience was seared in him, he had no thoughts of the great judgment-seat before which judges must appear. Though possibly he had taken an oath before God to judge impartially, yet he forgot his oath, and trod justice under his foot. "Neither did he regard man." The approbation of his fellow creatures, which is very often a power, even with naturally bad men, either to restrain them from overt evil, or else to constrain them to righteousness, this principle had no effect upon him. Now, if the widow prevailed over such a wretch as this, if the iron of her importunity broke the iron and steel of this man's obduracy, how much more may we expect to be successful with him who is righteous, and just, and good, the Friend of the needy, the Father of the fatherless, and the Avenger of all such as are oppressed! O let the character of God as it rises before you in all its majesty of truthfulness and faithfulness, blended with lovingkindness, and tenderness, and mercy, excite in you an indefatigable ardour of supplication, making you resolve with this poor woman that you will never cease to supplicate until you win your suit.

The judge was a man so unutterably bad, that he *even confessed his badness to himself*, with great contentment too. Without the slightest tinge of remorse, he said within himself, "Though I fear not God, neither regard man." There are few sinners who will go this length. They may neither fear God nor regard man, yet still they will indulge in their minds some semblance of that which is virtuous, and cheat themselves into the belief that at least they are not worse than other. But with this man there was no self-deception. He was as cool about his avowal as the Pharisee was concerning the opposite, "God, I thank thee that I am not as other men are." To what a brazen impertinence must this man have come, to what an extent must he have hardened his mind, that knowing himself to be such, he yet climbed the judgment-seat, and sat there to judge his fellow men! Yet the woman prevailed with this monster in human form, who had come to take pleasure in his own wickedness, and gloated in the badness of his own heart. Over this man importunity prevailed—how much more over him who spared not his own Son, but freely delivered him up for us all; how much more over him whose name is love, whose nature is everything that is attractive and encouraging to such as seek his face! The worse this judge appears, and he could scarcely have been painted in blacker colors, the more does the voice of the Savior seem to say to us, "Men ought always to pray, and not to faint."

Note with regard to the character of this judge, that he was one who *consciously cared for nothing but his own ease*. When at last he consented to do justice, the only motive which moved him, was, "lest by her continual coming she weary me." "She *stun* me," might be the Greek word—a kind of slang, I suppose, of that period, meaning lest "she batter me," "she bruise me," and as some translate it, "black my face with her incessant constant batterings." That was the kind of language he used; a short quick sentence of indignation at being bothered, as we should say, be such a case as this. The only thing that moved him was a desire to be at ease, and to take things comfortably. O brethren, if she could prevail over such a one, how much more shall we speed with God whose delight it is to take care of his children, who loves them even as the apple of his eye!

This judge was *practically unkind and cruel* to her; yet the widow continued. For awhile he would not listen to her, though her household, her life, her children's comfort, were all hanging upon his will; he left her by a passive injustice to suffer still. But our God has been practically kind and gracious to us, up to this moment he has heard us and granted our requests. Set this against the character of the judge, and surely every loving heart that knows the power of prayer will be moved to incessant importunity.

We must, however, pass on now to notice the other actor in the scene—*the widow;* and here everything tells again the same way, to induce the church of God to be importunate. She was apparently *a perfect stranger to the judge.* She appeared before him as an individual in whom he took no interest. He had possibly never seen her before; who she was and what she wanted as no concern to him. But when the church appears before God she comes as Christ's own bride, she appears before the Father as one whom he has loved with an everlasting love. And shall he not avenge his own elect, his own chosen, his own people? Shall not their prayers prevail with him, when a stranger's importunity won a suit of an unwilling judge?

The widow appeared at the judgement-seat *without a friend.* According to the parable, she had no advocate, no powerful pleader to stand up in the court and say, "I am the patron of this humble woman." If she prevailed, she must prevail by her own ardor and her own intensity of purpose. But when you and I come before our Father, we come not alone, for—

> "He is at the Father's side,
> The Man of love, the Crucified,"

We have a Friend who ever liveth to make intercession for us. O Christian, urge thy suit with holy boldness, press thy case, for the blood of Jesus speaks with a voice that must be heard. Be not thou therefore faint in thy spirit, but continue instant in thy supplication.

This poor woman came *without a promise to encourage her,* nay with the reverse, with much to discourage; but when you and I come before God, we are commanded to pray by God himself, and we are promised that if we ask it shall be given us, if we seek we shall find. Does she win without the sacred weapon of the promise, and shall not we win who can set the battering-rams of God's own word against the gates of heaven, a battering-ram that shall make every timber in those gates to quiver? O brethren, we must not pause nor cease a moment while we have God's promise to back our plea.

The widow, in addition to having no promise whatever, was even *without the right of constant access.* She had, I suppose, a right to clamor to be heard at ordinary times when judgment was administered, but what right had she to dog the judge's footsteps, to waylay him in the streets, to hammer at his private door, to be heard calling at nightfall, as that he, sleeping at the top of his house, was awakened by her cries? She had no permission so to importune, but we may come to God at all times and all seasons. We may cry day and night unto him, for he has bidden us pray without ceasing. What, without a permit is this woman so incessant! and with the sacred permissions which God has given us, and the encouragement of abounding lovingkindess, shall we cease to plead?

She, poor soul, every time she prayed, *provoked the judge;* lines of anger were on his face. I doubt not he foamed at the mouth to think he should be wearied by a person so insignificant; but with Jesus, every time we plead we please him rather than provoke him. The prayers of the saints are the music of God's ears.

> "To him there's music in a groan,
> And beauty in a tear."

We, speaking after the manner of men, bring a gratification to God when we intercede with him. He is vexed with us if we restrain our supplications; he is pleased with us when we draw near constantly. Oh, then, when you see the smile upon the Father's face, children of his love, I beseech you faint not, but continue still without ceasing to entreat the blessing.

Once more, this woman had a suit in which *the judge could not be himself personally interested;* but ours is a case in which the God we plead with is more interested than we are; for when a church asks for the conversion of souls, she may justly say, "Arise, O God, plead thine own cause," It is for the honor of Christ that souls should be converted; it brings glory to the mercy and power of God when great sinners are turned from the error of their ways; consequently we are pleading for the Judge with the Judge, for God we are pleading with God. Our prayer is virtually *for* Christ as *though* Christ, that his kingdom may come, and his will may be done.

I must not forget to mention that in this woman's case *she was only one.* She prevailed though she was only one, but shall not God avenge his own elect, who are not *one,* but tens of thousands? If there be a promise that if two or three are agreed it shall be done, how much more if in any church hundreds meet together with unanimous souls anxiously desiring that God would fulfill his promise? These pleas cast chains around the throne of God! How do they, as it were, hem in omnipotence! How they constrain the Almighty to arise out of his place and come in answer to his people, and do the great deed which shall bless his church and glorify himself.

You see, then, whether we consider the judge, or consider the widow, each character has points about it which tend to make us see our duty and our privilege to pray without ceasing.

The Power Which, According to This Parable, Triumphed

This power was not the woman's eloquence, "I pray thee avenge me of mine adversary." These words are very few. They have the merit of being very expressive, but he that would study oratory will not gather many lessons from them. "I pray thee avenge me of mine adversary.' Just eight words. You observe there is no plea, there is nothing about her widowhood, nothing urged about her children, nothing said about the wickedness of her adversary, nothing concerning the judgment of God upon unjust judges, nor about the wrath of God upon the unjust men, who devour widows' houses—nothing of the kind. "I pray thee avenge me of mine adversary." Her success, therefore, did not depend upon her power in rhetoric, and we learn from this that the prevalence of a soul or of a church with God does not rest upon the elocution of its words, or upon the eloquence of its language. The prayer which mounts to heaven may have but very few of the tail feathers of adornment about it, but it must have the strong wing feathers of intense desire; it must not be as the peacock, gorgeous for beauty, but it must be as the eagle, for soaring aloft, if it would ascend up to the seventh heaven. When you pray in public, as a rule the shorter the better. Words are cumbersome to prayer, It often happens that an abundance of words reveals a scarcity of desires. Verbiage is generally nothing better in prayer than a miserable fig leaf with which to cover the nakedness of an unawakened soul.

Another thing is quite certain, namely, that the woman *did not prevail through the merits of her case*. It may have been a very good case, there is nothing said about that. I do not doubt the rightness of it; but still, the judge did not know nor care whether it was right or wrong; all he cared about was, this woman troubled him. He does not say, "She has a good case, and I ought to listen to it." No, he was too bad a man to be moved by such a motive—but "she worries me," that is all, "I will attend to it." So in our suit—in the suit of a sinner with God, it is not the merit of his case that can ever prevail with God. Thou hast no merit. If thou art to win, another's merit must stand instead of thine, and on thy part it must not be merit but misery; it must not be thy righteousness but thy importunity that is to prevail with God. How this ought to encourage those of you who are laboring under a sense of prayer. Black may be the hand, but if it can but lift the knocker, the gate will open. Ay, though thou have a palsy in that hand; though, in addition to that palsy, thou be leprous, and the white leprosy be on thy forehead, yet if thou canst but tremblingly lift up that knocker and let it fall by its own weight upon that sacred promise, thou shalt surely get an audience with the King of kings. It is not eloquence, it is not merit, that wins with God, it is nothing but importunity.

Note with regard to this woman, that the judge said first, she troubled him, next he said, she came continually, and then he added his fear lest "she weary me." I think the case was somewhat after this fashion. The judge was sitting one morning on his bench, and many were the persons coming before him asking justice, which he was dealing out with the impartiality of a villain, giving always his best word to him who brought the heaviest bribes; when presently a poor woman uttered her plaint. She had tried to be heard several times, but her voice had been drowned by others, but this time it was more shrill and sharp, and she caught the judge's eye. "My lord, avenge me of mine adversary." He no sooner sees from her poverty-stricken dress that there are no bribes to be had, than he replies, "Hold your tongue! I have other business to attend to." He goes on with another suit in which the fees were more attractive. Still he hears the cry again, "My lord, I am a widow, avenge me of mine adversary," Vexed with the renewed disturbance, he bade the usher put her out, because she interrupted the silence of the court and stopped the public business. "Take care she does not get in again tomorrow," said he, "she is a troublesome woman." Long ere the morrow had come, he found out the truth of his opinion. She waited till he left the court, dogged his footsteps, and followed him through the streets, until he was glad to get through his door, and bade the servants fasten it lest that noisy widow should come in, for she had constantly assailed him with the cry, "Avenge me of mine adversary." He is now safely within doors, and bids the servants bring in his meal. They are pouring water on his hands and feet, his lordship is about to enjoy his repast, when a heavy knock is heard at the door, followed by a clamor, pushing, and a scuffle. "What is it?" saith he. "It is a woman outside, a widow woman, who wants your lordship to see justice done her." "Tell her I cannot attend to her, she must be gone." He seeks his rest at nightfall on the housetop, when he hears a heavy knock at the door, and a voice comes up from the street beneath his residence. "My lord, avenge me of mine adversary." The next morning his court is open, and, though she is forbidden to enter, like a dog that will enter somehow, she finds her way in, and she interrupts the court continually with her plea, "My lord, avenge me of mine adversary." Ask her why she is thus importunate, and she will tell you her husband is dead, and he left a little plot of land—it was all they had, and a cruel neighbor who looked with greedy eyes upon that little plot, had taken it as Ahab took Naboth's vineyard, and now she is without any meal or any oil for the little ones, and they are crying for food. Oh, if their father had been alive, how he would have guarded their interests! But she has no helper, and the case is a glaring one; and what is a judge for if he is not to protect the injured? She has no other chance, for the creditor is about to take away her children to sell them into bondage. She cannot bear that. "No," she says, "I have but one chance; it is that this man should speak up for me and do me justice, and I have made up my mind he shall never rest till he does so. I am resolved that if I perish, that the last words on my lips shall be, 'Avenge me of mine adversary.'" So the court is continually interrupted. Again the judge shouts, "Put her out; put her out! I cannot conduct the business at all with this crazy woman here continually dinning in my ears a shriek of 'Avenge me of mine adversary.'" But it is sooner said than done. She lays hold of the pillars of the court so as not to be dragged out, and when at last they grab her in the street, she does but wait her chance to enter again, she pursues the judge along the highways, she never lets him have a minute's peace. "Well," says the judge, "I am worried out of my very life. I care not for the widow, nor her property, nor her children; let them starve, what are they to me? But I cannot stand this, it will weary me beyond measure. I will see to it." It is done, and she goes her way. Nothing but her importunity prevails.

Now, brethren, you have many other weapons to use with God in prayer, but our Savior bids you not neglect this master, all-conquering, instrument of importunity. God will be more easily moved than this unjust judge, only be you as importunate as this widow was. If you are sure it is a right thing for which you are asking, plead now, plead at noon, plead at night, plead on; with cries and tears spread out your case, order your arguments, back up your pleas with reasons, urge the precious blood of Jesus, set the wounds of Christ before the Father's eyes, bring out the atoning sacrifice, point to Calvary, enlist the crowned Prince, the Priest who stands at the right hand of God; and resolve in your very soul that if Zion do not flourish, if souls be not saved, if your family be not blessed, if your own zeal be not revived, yet you will die with the plea upon your lips, and with the importunate wish upon your spirits. Let me tell you that if any of you should die with your prayers unanswered, you need not conclude that God had disappointed you. With one story I will finsih. I have heard that a certain godly father had the unhappiness to be the parent of some five or six most graceless sons. All of them as they grew up imbibed infidel sentiments, and led a libidinous life. The father who had been constantly praying for them, and was a pattern of every virtue, hoped at least that in his death he might be able to say a word that should move their heart. He gathered them to his bedside, but his unhappiness in dying was extreme, for he lost the light of God's countenance, and was beset with doubts and fears, and the last black thought that haunted him was, "Instead of my death being a testimony for God, which will win my dear sons, I die in such darkness and gloom that I fear I shall confirm them in their infidelity, and lead them to think that there is nothing in Christianity at all." The effect was the reverse. The sons came round the grave at the funeral, and when they returned to the house, the eldest son thus addressed his brothers:—"My brothers, throughout his lifetime, our father often spoke to us about religion, and we have always despised it, but what a sermon his deathbed had been to us! for if he who served God so well and lived so near to God found it so hard a thing to die, what kind of death may we expect ours to be who have lived without God and without hope?" The same feeling possessed them all, and thus the father's death had strangely answered the prayers of his life through the grace of God. You cannot tell but what, when you are in glory, you should look down from the windows of heaven and receive a double heaven in beholding your dear sons and daughters converted by the words you left behind. I do not say this to make you cease pleading for their immediate conversion, but to encourage you. Never give up prayer, never be tempted to cease from it. So long as there is breath in your body, and breath in their bodies, continue still to pray, for I tell you that he will avenge you speedily though he bear long with you. God bless these words for Jesus' sake. Amen.

10

*The Dream of Pilate's Wife**

When he was set down on the judgment seat, his wife sent unto him, saying, Have thou nothing to do with that just man: for I have suffered many things this day in a dream because of him (Matthew 27:19).

I earnestly wished to pursue the story of our Savior's trials previous to His crucifixion, but when I sat down to study the subject I found myself altogether incapable of the exercise. "When I thought to know this, it was too painful for me." My emotions grew so strong, and my sense of our Lord's grief became so extremely vivid, that I felt I must waive the subject for a time. I could not watch with Him another hour, and yet I could not leave the hallowed scene. It was therefore, a relief to meet with the episode of Pilate's wife and her dream: it enables me to continue the thread of my narrative, and yet to relax the extreme tension of the feelings caused by a near view of the Master's grief and shame. My spirit failed before the terrible sight. I thought I saw Him brought back from Herod where the men of war had set Him at nought. I followed Him through the streets again as the cruel priests pushed through the crowd and hastened Him back to Pilate's hall. I thought I heard them in the streets electing Barabbas, the robber, to be set free, instead of Jesus, the Savior, and I detected the first rising of that awful cry, "Crucify, crucify," which they shrieked out from their bloodthirsty throats: and there He stood, who loved me and gave Himself for me, like a lamb in the midst of wolves, with none to pity and none to help Him. The vision overwhelmed me, especially when I knew that the next stage would be that Pilate, who had exculpated Him by declaring, "I find no fault in Him," would give Him over to the tormentors that He might be scourged, that the mercenary soldiery would crown Him with thorns and mercilessly insult Him, and that He would be brought forth to the people and announced to them with that heart-rending word, "Behold

* This sermon was taken from *The Metropolitan Tabernacle Pulpit* and was preached on Sunday morning, February 26, 1882.

the man!" Was there ever sorrow like unto His sorrow? Rather than speak about it this day I feel inclined to act like Job's friends, of whom it is written, that at the sight of Him "they lifted up their voice, and wept; and sat down with him upon the ground seven days and seven nights, and none spake a word unto him: for they saw that his grief was very great."

We leave the Master awhile to look at this dream of Pilate's wife, which is only spoken of once in the Scriptures, and then by Matthew. I know not why that evangelist only should have been commissioned to record it; perhaps he alone heard of it; but the one record is sufficient for our faith, and long enough to furnish food for meditation. We receive the story as certified by the Holy Spirit.

Pilate throughout his term of office had grossly misbehaved himself. He had been an unjust and unscrupulous ruler of the Jews. The Galileans and the Samaritans both felt the terror of his arms; for he did not hesitate to massacre them at the slightest sign of revolt; and among the Jews themselves he had sent men with daggers into the midst of the crowds at the great gatherings, and so had cut off those who were obnoxious to him. Gain was his object, and pride ruled his spirit. At the time when Jesus of Nazareth was brought before him a complaint against him was on the way to Tiberius the Emperor, and he feared lest he should be called to account for his oppressions, extortions, and murders. His sins at this moment were beginning to punish him: as Job would word it, "The iniquities of his heels compassed him about." One terrible portion of the penalty of sin is its power to force a man to commit yet further iniquity. Pilate's transgressions were now howling around him like a pack of wolves; he could not face them, and he had not grace to flee to the one great refuge; but his fears drove him to flee before them, and there was no way apparently open for him but that which led him into yet deeper abominations. He knew that Jesus was without a single fault, and yet since the Jews clamored for His death he felt that he must yield to their demands, or else they would raise another accusation against himself namely, that he was not loyal to the sovereignty of Caesar, for he had allowed one to escape who had called Himself a king. If he had behaved justly he would not have been afraid of the chief priests and scribes. Innocence is brave; but guilt is cowardly. Pilate's old sins found him out and made him weak in the presence of the ignoble crew, whom otherwise he would have driven from the judgment seat. He had power enough to have silenced them, but he had not sufficient decision of character to end the contention: the power was gone from his mind because he knew that his conduct would not bear investigation, and he dreaded the loss of his office, which he held only for his own ends. See there with pity that scornful but vacillating creature wavering in the presence of men who were more wicked than himself and more determined in their purpose. The fell determination of the wicked priests caused hesitating policy to quail in their presence, and Pilate was driven to do what he would gladly have avoided.

The manner and the words of Jesus had impressed Pilate. I say the manner of Jesus, for His matchless meekness must have struck the governor as being a very unusual thing in a prisoner. He had seen in captured Jews the fierce courage of fanaticism; but there was no fanaticism in Christ. He had also seen in many prisoners the meanness which will do or say anything to escape from death; but he saw nothing of that about our Lord. He saw in Him unusual gentleness and humility combined with majestic dignity. He beheld submission blended with innocence. This made Pilate feel how awful goodness is. He was impressed—he could not help being impressed—with this unique sufferer. Besides, our Lord had before him witnessed a good confession—you remember how we considered it the other day—and though Pilate had huffed it off with the pert question, "What is truth?" and had gone back into the judgment hall, yet there was an arrow fixed within him which he could not shake off. It may have been mainly superstition; but he felt an awe of One whom he half suspected to be an extraordinary personage. He felt that he himself was placed in a very extraordinary position, being asked to condemn One who he knew to be perfectly innocent. His duty was clear enough, he could never have had a question about that; but duty was nothing to Pilate in comparison with his own interests. He would spare the Just One if he could do so without endangering himself; but his cowardly fears lashed him on to the shedding of innocent blood.

At the very moment when he was vacillating, when he had proffered to the Jews the choice of Barabbas, or Jesus of Nazareth—at that very moment, I say, when he had taken his seat upon the bench, and was waiting for their choice, there came from the hand of God a warning to him, a warning which would forever make it clear that, if he condemned Jesus, it would be done voluntarily by his own guilty hands. Jesus must die by the determinate counsel and foreknowledge of God, and yet it must be by wicked hands that He is crucified and slain; and hence Pilate must not sin in ignorance. A warning to Pilate came from his own wife concerning her morning's dream, a vision of mystery and terror, warning him not to touch that just person; "for," said she, "I have suffered many things this day in a dream because of him." There are times in most men's lives when, though they have been wrong, yet they have not quite been set on mischief, but have come to a pause and have deliberated as to their way; and then God in great mercy has sent them a caution, and has set up a danger-signal bidding them stop in their mad career ere they plunged themselves finally into irretrievable ruin. Somewhere in that direction lies the subject of our present discourse. O that the Spirit of God may make it useful to many.

The Cooperation of Providence with the Work of God

And, first, I call your attention to THE COOPERATION OF PROVIDENCE WITH THE WORK OF GOD. I call it the work of God to warn men against sin, and I call your attention to Providence working with it to bring the preventives and cautions of divine mercy home to men's minds.

For, first, observe the providence of God *in sending this dream*. If anything beneath the moon may be thought to be exempt from law, and to be the creature of pure chance, surely it is a dream. True, there were in old time dreams in which God spoke to men prophetically; but ordinarily they are the carnival of thought, a maze of mental states, a dance of disorder. The dreams which would naturally come to the wife of a Roman governor would not be likely to have much of tenderness or conscience in them, and would not, in all probability, of themselves run in the line of mercy. Dreams ordinarily are the most disorderly of phenomena, and yet it seems that they are ordered of the Lord. I can well understand that every drop of spray which flashes from the wave when it dashes against the cliff has its appointed orbit as truly as the stars of heaven; but the thoughts of men appear to be utterly lawless, especially the thoughts of men when deep sleep falls upon them. As well might one foretell the flight of a bird as the course of a dream. Such wild fantasies seem to be ungoverned and ungovernable. Many things operate naturally to fashion a dream. Dreams frequently depend upon the condition of the stomach, upon the meat and drink taken by the sleeper before going to rest. They often owe their shape to the state of the body or the agitation of the mind. Dreams may, no doubt, be caused by that which transpires in the chamber of the house; a little movement of the bed caused by passing wheels, or the tramp of a band of men, or the passing of a domestic across the floor, or even the running of a mouse behind the wainscot, may suggest and shape a dream. Any slight matter affecting the senses at such time may raise within the slumbering mind a mob of strange ideas. Yet whatever may have operated in this lady's case, the hand of providence was in it all, and her mind, though fancy free, wandered nowhere but just according to the will of God, to elect the divine purpose. She must dream just so, and no how else, and that dream must be of such and such an order, and none other. Even dreamland knows no god but God, and even phantoms and shadows come and go at His bidding, neither can the images of a night-vision escape from the supreme authority of the Most High. See the providence of God in the fact that the dream of Pilate's wife, however caused, should be of such a form and come at such a time as this. Certain old writers trace her dream to the devil, who thus hoped to prevent the death of our Lord, and so prevent our redemption. I do not agree with the notion; but even if it were so, I admire all the more the providence which overrules even the devices of Satan for the purposes of wisdom. Pilate must be warned, so that his sentence may be his own act and deed, and that warning is given him through his wife's dream. So does Providence work.

Note, next, the providence of God in arranging that *with this dream there should be great mental suffering*. "I have suffered many things in a dream concerning him!" I cannot tell what vision passed before her mind's eye, but it was one which caused her terrible agony. A modern artist has painted a picture of what he imagined the dream to be, but I shall not attempt to follow that great man in the exercise of fancy. Pilate's wife may have realized in her sleep the dreadful spectacle of the thorn-crown and the scourge, or even of the crucifixion and the death-agony; and truly I know of nothing more calculated to make the heart suffer many things concerning the Lord Jesus than a glance at His death. Around the cross there gathers grief enough to cause many a sleepless night, if the soul has any tenderness left in it. Or her dream may have been of quite another kind. She may have seen in vision the Just One coming in the clouds of heaven. Her mind may have pictured Him upon the great white throne, even the man whom her husband was about to condemn to die. She may have seen her husband brought forth to judgment, himself a prisoner to be tried by the Just One, who had aforetime been accused before him. She may have awoke, startled at the shriek of her husband as he fell back into the pit that knows no bottom. Whatever it was, she had suffered repeated painful emotions in the dream, and she awoke startled and amazed. The terror of the night was upon her, and it threatened to become a terror to her for all her days, and she therefore hastens to stay her husband's hand. Now, herein is the hand of God, and the simple story goes to prove that the wandering Zingari of dreamland are still under His control, and He can cause them to produce distress and anguish, if some grand end is to be served thereby.

Equally remarkable is it that *she should have sent to her husband the message*, "Have nothing to do with this just person." Most dreams we quite forget; a few we mention as remarkable, and only now and then one is impressed upon us so that we remember it for years. Scarcely have any of you had a dream which made you send a message to a magistrate upon the bench. Such an intention would only be resorted to in an urgent case. Though the judge were your own husband you would be very hard pressed before you would worry him with your dreams while he was occupied with important public business. Mostly a dream may wait until business is over. But so deep was the impression upon this Roman lady's mind that she does not wait until her lord comes home, but sends to him at once. Her advice is urgent—"Have thou nothing to do with this Just One." She must warn him now, before he has laid a stroke on Him, much less imbrued his hands in His blood. Not "have a little to do and scourge Him, and let Him go," but "have thou nothing to do with Him. Say not an unkind word, nor do Him any injury! Deliver Him from His adversaries! If He must die, let it be by some other hand than yours! My husband, my husband, my husband, I beseech you, have nothing to do with this just Person. Let Him alone, I pray you!" She words her message very emphatically. "Have nothing to do with this just Person: for I have suffered many things in a dream concerning Him. Think of your wife! Think of yourself! Let my sufferings about this Holy One be a warning to you. For my sake let Him alone!" And yet, do you know, her message to my ear sounds rather authoritative for a woman to her husband, and he a judge! There is a tone about it that is not ordinarily in the address of wives to husbands. "Have thou nothing to do with that just man: for I have suffered many things this day in a dream because of him." It shows a wonderful providence of God that this lady was moved to send so strong a message to her self-willed husband, to beseech, to entreat, to implore, almost to demand of him, that he let this just Man go. O Providence, how mightily can you work! O Lord, the seraphim obey you, but you find an equally willing servitor in a wife who, at your bidding, stands between her husband and a crime.

Once more, about this providence I want you to notice *the peculiar time in which her warning came*. It was evidently a dream of the morning: "I have suffered many things in a dream this day." The day had not long broken—it was yet early in the morning. The Romans had a superstition that morning dreams are true. I suppose it was after her husband had left her that she thus dreamed. If I may be allowed, not to state a fact, but to make a conjecture, which seems to me most probable, she was a dearly beloved wife, but sickly, and therefore needed to rest further into the day than her husband; and when he had left his couch she had yet another sleep, and being a sensitive person, and all the more likely to dream, she awoke from her morning sleep oppressed with a terror which she could not shake off. Pilate was gone, and she was told that he was in the judgment hall. She asked her attendants why he was there so early, and they replied that there had been an unusual clamor in the courtyard, for the high priests and a mob of Jews had been there, and the governor had gone out to them. They might, perhaps, also tell her that Jesus of Nazareth was brought there a prisoner, and the priests were entreating Pilate to put Him to death, though they had heard the governor say that he found no fault in Him. "Go," she said to her maid, "call to one of the guards, and bid him go at once to my husband, and say what I tell you. Let him speak aloud, that some of the cruel Jews may hear it, and be moved from their cruel purpose: let him say that I implore my husband to have nothing to do with this just Person, for I have suffered many things this very morning in a dream concerning Him." Just at the moment, you see, when he had sat down on the judgment seat, the warning came to him. When there was a little lull, and he was anxious to acquit his prisoner, at that instant of time which was the most hopeful this weight was thrown into the right side of the scale, thrown in most wisely and mercifully to keep back Pilate from his grievous sin. The warning came at the nick of time, as we say, though, alas, it came in vain! Admire the punctuality of Providence. God never is before His time; He never is too late. It shall be seen concerning all that He does that on the selfsame day determined by the prophecy the fulfillment came. My soul stands trembling while she sings the glory of her God, whose providence is high, even like Ezekiel's wheels; but the wheels are full of eyes, and, as they turn, all the surroundings are observed and provided for, so that there are no slips, or oversights, or accidents or delays. Prompt and effectual is the operation of the Lord.

Thus much concerning Providence, and I think you will all agree that my point is proven—that providence is always co-working with the grace of God. A great writer who knows but little about divine things, yet, nevertheless, tells us that he perceives a power in the world which works for righteousness. Exactly so it is well spoken, for this is the chief of all powers. When you and I go out to warn men of sin, we are not alone, all Providence is at our back. When we preach Christ crucified, we are workers together with God; God is working with us as well as by us. Everything that happens is driving toward the end for which we work, when we seek to convince men of sin and of righteousness. Where the Spirit of God is, all the forces of nature and providence are mustered. The fall of empires, the death of despots, the uprise of nations, the making or the breaking of treaties, terrific wars and blighting famines, are all working out the grand end. Yea, and domestic matters, such as the death of children, the sickness of wives, the loss of work, the poverty of the family, and a thousand other things are working, working, ever working, for the improvement of men; and you and I, lending our poor feebleness to cooperate with God, are marching with all the forces of the universe. Have comfort, then, in this. O workers for Jesus, suffering many things for Him, be of good courage, for the stars in their courses fight for the servants of the living God, and the stones of the field are in league with you.

The Accessibility of Conscience to God

Secondly, I gather from this story THE ACCESSIBILITY OF CONSCIENCE TO GOD. How are we to reach Pilate? How are we to give him warning? He has rejected the voice of Jesus and the sight of Jesus—could not Peter be fetched to expostulate with him? Alas, he has denied his Master. Could not John be brought in? Even he has forsaken the Lord. Where shall a messenger be found? It shall be found in a dream. God can get at men's hearts, however hardened they may be. Never give them up, never despair of arousing them. If my ministry, your ministry, and the ministry of the blessed Book should all seem to be nothing, God can reach the conscience by a dream. If the sword comes not at them at close quarters, yet what seems but a stray arrow from a bow drawn at a venture shall find out the joints in their harness. We ought to believe in God about wicked men, and never say of them, "It is impossible that they should be converted." The Lord can wound leviathan, for His weapons are many, and they are suited to the foe. I do not think a dream would operate upon *my* mind to convince me; but certain minds lie open in that direction, and to them a dream may be a power. God may use even superstition to accomplish His beneficent purposes. Many besides Pilate have been warned by dreams.

Better still, Pilate was accessible through the dream *of his wife*. Henry Melvill has a very wonderful discourse upon this topic, in which he tries to show that probably if Pilate had dreamed this dream himself it would not have been so operative upon him as when his wife dreamed it. He takes it as a supposition, which nobody can deny, that Pilate had an affectionate and tender wife, who was very dear to him. The one brief narrative which we have of her certainly looks that way; it is evident that she loved her husband dearly, and would therefore prevent his acting unjustly to Jesus. To send a warning by her was to reach Pilate's conscience through his affections. If his beloved wife was distressed it would be sure to weigh heavily with him: for he would not have her troubled. He would fain shield his tender one from every breath of wind and give her perfect comfort, and when she pleads it is his delight to yield. It is, therefore, no small trouble to him that she is suffering, suffering so much as to send a message to him, suffering because of one who deserves her good opinion—one whom he himself knows to be without fault. If this lady was indeed the wife of Pilate's youth, tender and dearly beloved, and if she was gradually sickening before his eyes, her pale face would rise before his loving memory, and her words would have boundless power over him when she said, "I have suffered many things in a dream." O Claudia Procula, if that were your name, well did the Lord of mercy entrust His message to your persuasive lips, for from you it would come with tenfold influence. Tradition declares this lady to have been a Christian, and the Greek church have placed her in their calendar as a saint. For this we have no evidence; all that we know is that she was Pilate's wife, and used her wifely influence to stay him from this crime. How often has a tender, suffering, loving woman exercised great power over a coarse, rough man! The All-wise One knows this, and hence He often speaks to sinful men by this influential agency. He converts one in a family that she may be His missionary to the rest. Thus He speaks with something better than the tongues of men and of angels, for He uses love itself to be His orator. Affection has more might than eloquence. That is why, my friend, God sent you for a little while that dear child who prattled to you about the Savior. She is gone to heaven now, but the music of her little hymns rings in your ear even now, and her talk about Jesus and the angels is yet with you. She has been called home; but God sent her to you for a season to charm you to Himself and win you to the right way. Thus He bade you cease from sin and turn to Christ. And that dear mother of yours, who is now before the throne, do you remember what she said to you when she was dying? You have heard me a great many times, but you never heard a sermon from me like that address from her dying couch. You can never quite forget it, or shake yourself free from its power. Beware how you trifle with it. To Pilate his wife's message was God's ultimatum; He warned him never again, and even Jesus stood silent before him. O my friend, to you it may be that your child, your mother, or your affectionate wife may be God's last messenger, the final effort of the warning angel to bring you to a better mind. A loving relative pleading with tears is often the forlorn hope of mercy. An attack so skillfully planned and wisely conducted may be regarded as the last assault of love upon a stubborn spirit, and after this it will be left to its own devices. The selection of the wife was no doubt made by infinite wisdom and tenderness, that if possible Pilate might be arrested in his career of crime and strengthened to the performance of an act of justice by which he would have avoided the most terrible of crimes.

So, then, we may safely conclude that the Lord has His missionaries where the city missionary cannot enter; He sends the little children to sing and pray where the preacher is never heard; He moves the godly woman to proclaim the gospel by her lip and life where the Bible is not read. He sends a sweet girl to grow up and win a brother or a father where no other voice would be allowed to tell of Jesus and His love. We thank God it is so; it gives hope for the households of this godless city, it gives us hope even for those for whom the Sabbath-bell rings out in vain. They will hear, they must hear these home preachers, these messengers who tug at their hearts.

Ay, and let me add that where God does not employ a dream, nor use a wife, yet He can get at men's conscience by no visible means but *by thoughts which come unbidden and abide upon the soul.* Truths long buried suddenly rise up, and when the man is in the very act of sin he is stopped in the way, as Balaam was when the angel met him. How often it has happened that conscience has met a guilty man even in the moment when he meant to enjoy the pleasure bought with wrong, even as Elijah met Ahab at the gate of Naboth's vineyard! How the king starts back as he beholds the prophet: he would sooner have seen the very fiend than Elijah. Angrily he cries, "Hast thou found me, O mine enemy?" Though, indeed, Elijah was his best friend, had he known it. Often does conscience pounce upon a man when the sweet morsel of sin has just been rolled under his tongue, and he is sitting down to enjoy it: the visitation of conscience turns the stolen honey into bitterness, and the forbidden joy into anguish. Conscience often lies like a lion in a thicket, and when the sinner comes along the broad road it leaps upon him, and for a while he is sorely put to it. The bad man is comparable to leviathan, of whom we read that his scales are his pride, shut up together as with a close seal; so that the sword of him that lays at him cannot hold, the spear, the dart, nor the javelin; and yet the Lord has a way of coming at him and of sore wounding him. Let us, therefore, both hope and pray for the very worst of men.

Brothers and sisters, use for the good of men anything which comes in your way. Use not only sober argument and sound doctrine, but even if a dream has touched your heart, do not hesitate to repeat it where it may have effect. Any weapon may be used in this war. but see to it that you do seek the souls of men, all of you. You who are wives should be especially stirred up to this sacred work. Remember Pilate's wife, and think of her as affectionately giving the warning to her husband, and go and do likewise. Never keep back from an ungodly husband the word which may convert him from the error of his ways. And you, dear children, you sisters, you of the gentler sort, do not hesitate, in your own quiet way, to be heralds for Jesus wherever your lot is cast. As for us all, let us take care that we use every occasion for repressing sin and creating holiness. Let us warn the ungodly at once; for perhaps the man to whom we are sent has not yet performed the fatal deed. Let us stand in the gap while yet there is space for repentance. Pilate is even now sitting on the judgment seat. Time is precious. Make haste! Make haste, ere yet he commits the deed of blood! Send the messenger to him! Stop him ere the deed is done; even though he should complain of your interference. Say to him, "Have nothing to do with this just Person: for I have suffered many things because of Him, and I pray you do nothing against Him."

That is our second point. God bless it; although I cannot preach upon it as I would, the Spirit of God can put power into it.

The Frequent Failure Even of the Best Means

Thirdly, we have now the lamentable task of observing THE FREQUENT FAILURE EVEN OF THE BEST MEANS. I have ventured to say that, humanly speaking, it was the best means of reaching Pilate's conscience for his wife to be led to expostulate with him. He would hear but few, but her he would hear; and yet even her warning was in vain. What was the reason?

First, *self-interest* was involved in the matter, and that is a powerful factor. Pilate was afraid of losing his governorship. The Jews would be angry if he did not obey their cruel bidding; they might complain to Tiberius, and he would lose his lucrative position. Alas, such things as these are holding some of you captives to sin at this moment. You cannot afford to be true and right, for it would cost too much. You know the will of the Lord; you know what is right; but you renounce Christ by putting Him off, and by abiding in the ways of sin that you may gain the wages thereof. You are afraid that to be a true Christian would involve the loss of a friend's goodwill, or the patronage of an ungodly person, or the smile of an influential worldling, and this you cannot afford. You count the cost, and reckon that it is too high. You resolve to gain the world, even though you lose your soul! What then? You will go to hell rich! A sorry result this! Do you see anything desirable in such an attainment? Oh that you would consider your ways and listen to the voice of wisdom!

The next reason why his wife's appeal was ineffectual was the fact that Pilate was *a coward*. A man with legions at his back, and yet afraid of a Jewish mob—afraid to let one poor prisoner go whom he knew to be innocent; afraid because he knew his conduct would not bear inspection! He was, morally, a coward! Multitudes of people go to hell because they have not the courage to fight their way to heaven. "The fearful and unbelieving shall have their portion in the lake which burneth with fire and brimstone, which is the second death." So says the Word of God. They are afraid of encountering a fool's laugh, and so rush upon everlasting contempt. They could not bear to tear themselves away from old companions, and excite remarks and sarcasm among ungodly wits, and so they keep their companions and perish with them. They have not the pluck to say "No," and swim against the stream; they are such cowardly creatures that they will sooner be forever lost than face a little scorn.

Yet while there was cowardice in Pilate, there was *presumption* too. He who was afraid of man and afraid to do right, yet dared to incur the guilt of innocent blood. Oh, the cowardice of Pilate to take water and wash his hands, as if he could wash off blood with water; and then to say, "I am innocent of his blood"—which was a lie—"see ye to it." By those last words he brought the blood upon himself, for he consigned his prisoner to their tender mercies, and they could not have laid a hand upon Him unless He had given them leave. Oh, the daring of Pilate thus in the sight of God to commit murder and disclaim it. There is a strange mingling of cowardliness and courage about many men; they are afraid of a man, but not afraid of the eternal God who can destroy both body and soul in hell. This is why men are not saved, even when the best of means are used, because they are presumptuous, and dare defy the Lord.

Besides this, Pilate was *double-minded*: he had a heart and a heart. He had a heart after that which was right, for he sought to release Jesus; but he had another heart after that which was gainful, for he would not run the risk of losing his post by incurring the displeasure of the Jews. We have plenty around us who are double-minded. Such are here this morning; but where were they last night? You will be touched by today's sermon! How will you be affected tomorrow by a lewd speech or a lascivious song? Many men run two ways; they seem earnest about their souls, but they are far more eager after gain or pleasure. Strange perversity of man that he should tear himself in two. We have heard of tyrants tying men to wild horses and dragging them asunder, but these people do this with themselves. They have too much conscience to neglect the Sabbath, and to forego attendance at the house of prayer; too much conscience to be utterly irreligious, to be honestly infidel; and yet at the same time they have not enough conscience to keep them from being hypocrites. They let "I dare not" wait upon "I would." They want to do justly, but it would be too costly. They dare not run risks, and yet, meanwhile, they run the awful risk of being driven forever from the presence of God to the place where hope can never come. Oh that my words were as from a culverin! Oh that they would hurl a cannon-shot at indecision! Oh that I could speak like God's own thunder, which makes the hinds to calve, and breaks the rocks in pieces: even so would I warn men against these desperate evils which thwart the efforts of mercy, so that, even when the man's own wife, with the most tender love, bids him escape from the wrath to come, he still chooses his own destruction.

The Overwhelming Condemnation of Those Who Thus Transgress

Lastly, we have a point which is yet more terrible, THE OVERWHELMING CONDEMNATION OF THOSE WHO THUS TRANSGRESS. This Pilate was guilty beyond all excuse. He deliberately and of his own free will condemned the just Son of God to die, being informed that He was the Son of God, and knowing both from his own examination and from his wife that He was a "just Person."

Observe that the message which he received was most distinct. It was suggested by a dream; but there is nothing dreamy about it. It is as plain as words can be put—"Have thou nothing to do with that just man: for I have suffered many things this day in a dream because of him." He condemned the Lord with his eyes open, and that is an awful way of sinning. Oh, my dear friends, am I addressing any here who are purposing to do some very sinful thing, but have lately received a warning from God? I would add one more caution. I pray you by the blessed God, and by the bleeding Savior, and as you love yourself, and as you love her from whom the warning may have come to you, do stop, and hold your hand! Do not this abominable thing! You know better. The warning is not put to you in some mysterious and obscure way; but it comes point blank to you in unmistakable terms. God has sent conscience to you, and He has enlightened that conscience, so that it speaks very plain English to you. This morning's discourse stops you on the highway of sin, puts its pistol to your ear, and demands that you "Stand and deliver." Stir an inch, and it will be at your own soul's peril. Do you hear me? Will you regard the heaven-sent expostulation? Oh, that you would stand still awhile and hear what God shall speak while He bids you yield yourself to Christ today. It may be *now or never* with you, as it was with Pilate that day. He had the evil thing which he was about to do fully described to him, and therefore if he ventured on it, his presumption would be great. His wife had not said, "Have nothing to do with this man," but "with this *just* man," and that word rang in his ears, and again and again repeated itself until he repeated it too. Read the twenty-fourth verse. When he was washing his wicked hands he said, "I am innocent of the blood of this just Person"—the very name his wife had given to our Lord. The arrows stuck in him! He could not shake them off! Like a wild beast, he had the javelin sticking in his side, and though he rushed into the forest of his sin, it was evidently rankling in him still—"that just Person" haunted him. Sometimes God makes a man see sin as sin, and makes him see the blackness of it; and if he then perseveres in it, he becomes doubly guilty, and pulls down upon himself a doom intolerable beyond that of Sodom of old.

Beside that, Pilate was sinning not only after distinct warning, and a warning which set out the blackness of the sin, but he was sinning after his conscience had been touched and moved through his affections. It is a dreadful thing to sin against a mother's prayer. She stands in your way; she stretches out her arms, with tears she declares that she will block your road to perdition. Will you force your way to ruin over her prostrate form? She kneels! She grasps your knees, she begs you not to be lost. Are you so brutal as to trample on her love? Your little child entreats you; will you disregard her tears? Alas, she was yours, but death has removed her, and ere she departed she entreated you to follow her to heaven and she sang her little hymn—

> Yes, we'll gather at the river.

Will you fling your babe aside as though you were another Herod that would slay the innocents, and all in order that you may curse yourself forever and be your own destroyer? It is hard for me to talk to you thus. If it is coming home to any of you it will be very hard for you to hear it; indeed, I hope it will be so hard that you will end it by saying, "I will yield to love which assails me by such tender entreaties."

It will not be a piece of mere imagination if I conceive that at the last great day, when Jesus sits upon the judgment seat, and Pilate stands there to be judged for the deeds done in the body, that his wife will be a swift witness against him to condemn him. I can imagine that at the last great day there will be many such scenes as that, wherein those who loved us best will bring the most weighty evidences against us, if we are still in our sins. I know how it affected me as a lad when my mother, after setting before her children the way of salvation, said to us, "If you refuse Christ and perish, I cannot plead in your favor and say that you were ignorant. No, but I must say Amen to your condemnation." I could not bear *that!* Would my mother say "Amen" to my condemnation? And yet, Pilate's wife, what can you do otherwise? When all must speak the truth, what can you say but that your husband was tenderly and earnestly warned by you and yet consigned the Savior to His enemies?

Oh, my ungodly hearers, my soul goes out after you. "Turn, turn, why will you die?" Why will you sin against the Savior? God grant you may not reject your own salvation, but may turn to Christ and find eternal redemption in Him. "Whosoever believeth in him hath everlasting life."

11

*Magdalene at the Sepulcher: An Instructive Scene**

"Then the disciples went away again unto their own home. But Mary stood without at the sepulcher weeping: and as she wept, she stooped down, and looked into the sepulcher, and seeth two angels in white sitting, the one at the head, and the other at the feet, where the body of Jesus had lain. And they say unto her, Woman, why weepest thou? She saith unto them, Because they have taken away my Lord, and I know not where they have laid him. And when she had thus said, she turned herself back, and saw Jesus standing, and knew not that it was Jesus. Jesus saith unto her, Woman, why weepest thou? whom seekest thou? She, supposing him to be the gardener, saith unto him, Sir, if thou have borne him hence, tell me where thou hast laid him, and I will take him away. Jesus said unto her, Mary. She turned herself, and saith uuto him, Rabboni; which is to say, Master (John 20:10–16).

I wanted to speak tonight to believers who have lost the joyful presence of their Lord, and who are saying, "Oh, that I knew where I might find Him!" But when I thought of that matter, I said to myself, Many will be in the congregation who have never yet found Him, and therefore do not know His sweetness by experience, and yet they may be longing to find Him. Is it possible to benefit two classes at once? "Well, well," I said to myself, "I can speak to the saint, for she who figures in the text was Mary; but I can also, at the same time, talk to the sinner; for she was Magdalene, and that name has somehow become connected with penitent sinners." I pray, at the beginning, that, if there be one here who has long been a Mary, and has followed Christ lovingly, and if there be another here

* This sermon was taken from *The Metropolitan Tabernacle Pulpit* and was preached on Thursday evening, October 24, 1889.

who is more like what is commonly, but erroneously, known as a Magdalene, both the Mary and the Magdalene may find direction and consolation in my discourse.

I shall have no other preface but these remarks; for we have before us a long text to be handled in a short time, and I would not perform my task slightingly. We will advance by a series of observations.

A Soul Seeking Jesus Has Ways of Its Own

Read carefully the tenth verse: "Then the disciples went away again unto their own home. *But Mary*," Mary had her own way of proceeding. Mary was seeking Christ more intensely and affectionately than even the choicest of the apostles. They were more able to wait for events than her eagerness would allow her to do. John was able to go home, because he had seen and believed. Peter went home all the more readily because a cloud darkened his sky. Mary was of another order from either of these: she loved, and longed to see Him whom she loved. Whether He be dead or alive, she would find Him. When you are seeking the Lord, it brings out your individuality. Every truly anxious soul must seek the Lord in His own way. Each case is peculiar: each seeker feels himself to be one by himself. There are not two Mary Magdalenes; and Mary differs from John and Peter.

One part of her way was this—that *she would stay at the sepulcher after others had gone to their own homes*. So have I seen the lover of the Lord lingering at the mercy seat when the prayers of others were ended, and remaining in the use of the means of grace when others had enjoyed a full sufficiency of them. The meeting is very early in the morning, but Mary must be there; and if the meeting be at a distance, she trudges over the miles. One saint is noted for Bible reading, and nothing will attract her from it. Another abounds in private prayer, and is mighty on her knees. Another feels bound to go where Christ Jesus is earnestly talked about, and therefore he spends many an hour with the Lord's people. Perhaps Peter and John had other necessary business to attend to, and their duty called them away from the tomb; but Mary stood there still, hoping to hear something about her Lord, and, at least, to know where they had laid His body. It is a blessed thing when the heart becomes so resolved to find Christ that it cannot be happy without Him, cannot even live without Him. When you are resolved to wait at the posts of wisdom's doors until the Incarnate Wisdom appears to you, you will not have to wait long.

Mary had ways of her own beside, for she stood there "weeping." I do not read that, upon this occasion, either Peter or John shed a single tear. They may have done so, but the Holy Spirit has not recorded the fact; yet He has recorded it of this earnest seeker that she "stood without at the sepulcher weeping." She wept as if her heart would break. Where was her

Lord? What had they done with that sacred body? She had seen it wrapped in spices and fine linen, and laid in the tomb of Joseph; where was it now? The tomb was evidently quite empty of all but the cerements; where was the body? What new indignities had the cruel ones put upon it? That dear mangled body—to what malicious treatment was it now exposed? She stood, in deep emotion, sorrowing as love alone can sorrow when its beloved object is in peril. It is a great thing, dear soul, when you cannot find Christ, to weep your eyes out until you can. When you cannot live without Him for very heartbreak; when all the joy of life is gone; when existence becomes only another name for grieving after an absent love, and that love the Lord Jesus; then you are not far off from the happy hour of finding Him. Tears may be as the dew of the morning, the sure prophets of the rising sun. At any rate, many search for Jesus with tears in their eyes.

Mary did something more, which was according to her own mode of action—"*she stooped down, and looked into the sepulcher*." They that would find Christ must stoop to look for Him. They must not merely wait for Him, but look for Him on their knees. I have known some people pretend to wait for the Lord, and they have kept up the pretense to their soul's ruin! for they never looked to Him by faith. I have known some weep much, but they would not open their eyes to look to Jesus and be saved. True seekers look for Jesus in the Scriptures; they search for Him in the hearing of the Word; they cry after Him in their private rooms. This is well. If you would be saved, seek Jesus, and He will find you. Cry evermore, "Oh, that I knew where I might find Him! I would come even to His seat." No heart has ever yet earnestly looked after Jesus but what before long He has been seen. If there be this waiting, this weeping, this stooping, this looking, there will be an appearing in mercy, and a recognition in joy. Mary, who looks for Jesus, shall see Him.

Note this peculiarity: that she looked in the wrong place. She looked into the sepulcher for the living and risen Jesus. Earnest, true-hearted, zealous, Mary was; but she labored under a mistake. Well might the angels say, "Why seek ye the living among the dead? He is not here, but is risen." Thus have I known true penitents seek the Lord where He cannot be found. They have expected to undergo a sort of inward purgatory, and they have sought for Jesus in their own feelings. He is not there. They have imagined that they must be carried away with despair before they might lay hold upon the Savior. Yet the Lord is not in the wind of feeling, nor in the fire of despair: His presence is known by His still small voice. They have not looked with a simple, childlike trust to Jesus; but have gone about to this, and that, and the other thing, and all in vain. They have sought for Jesus among forms and ceremonies, but in vain. Possibly they have gone to human priests, or sages: these are as dead as the tombs. Priestcraft and philosophy are no places for the living Christ to be found in.

Yet I am glad that Mary looked into the tomb; for, though she looked in the wrong place, it was a good thing to be looking for Jesus after any fashion. Better blunder in seeking Christ than be so wise as to go away from Him. I mean, better to be a sincere, but foolish, seeker after Jesus, and fall into a hundred errors of doctrine, than to be highly cultured, and all the while to be looking to self, or to the world, and forgetting the Lord Jesus. Poor seekers! you are in trouble, I see it by your tears. There is hope for you, for you have eyes, and are looking out for something better than you can find in yourselves, or in your fellow men. I am sure of you, for you will not run away home; you stay near the place where Jesus was last seen. You are not rolling stones, but you abide in earnest hearing, in apostolic doctrine, and in prayers. Your constancy and your eagerness are cheering signs that grace is beginning its work in your hearts. Comfort is on the way to you, I can see the light of it reflected in those tears which glisten in your eyes. God grant that we may not be disappointed in you, for His name's sake!

A Soul Seeking Jesus Makes Small Account of Anything Else

Mary, when she looked down, saw the angels sitting, the one at the head, and the other at the feet, where the body of Jesus had lain. At any other time, if Mary Magdalene had seen two angels, she would have been astounded, so as to lose her balance, through reverent fear. A vision of angels to a holy woman—there is something overpowering in it. A vision of angels, even to the ungodly soldiers that watched the grave of Christ, had made them faint, and become as dead men; but if you read the passage attentively, you will see that Mary talked to these angels as if they had been good men whom she had met before. She was not abashed by them. When they say to her, "Woman, why weepest thou?" she answers them, very plainly, "Because they have taken away my Lord, and I know not where they have laid him." She is not frightened at spirits and angels. *Neither is a soul that is in earnest after Christ to be put away from its search by any sort of diversion.* The true inquirer would ask of angels, or of the most eminent saints, concerning the Lord Jesus. It will be only too glad to ask of anybody, or to answer a question from anybody, if it may thus hope to find Jesus. Did you never note the all-subduing power of a great desire? When God makes the heart tender, and sets it longing after Jesus, it forgets its own feebleness, and ceases to be alarmed by that which once distressed it. A longing soul would break through angels and through devils, through heaven and through earth, to reach Jesus. We must have Him. We must behold the Well-beloved. Our soul is all on fire for Him, it cannot be restrained, it will burn its way to Him as the flame makes its way across the prairie. We want Jesus, and we will not be content with anything short of Him.

Notice, too, as confirmatory of what I have said, that *when a soul is seeking Christ, nothing but Christ's own Word will satisfy it.* This holy woman was not content with what the angels said. Though they said to her, "Woman, why weepest thou?" Those shining ones do not appear to have comforted her at all. She went on weeping. She told them why she wept, but she did not, therefore, cease her tears. And, believe me, if the angels of heaven cannot content a heart which is seeking after Jesus, you may depend upon it that the angels of the churches cannot do so. We may preach as best we can, but the words of man will never satisfy the cravings of the heart. The seeker needs Jesus: Jesus only, but Jesus certainly. You read the best of books, and heard the most faithful of testimonies when you were seeking, and yet you came away, and cried, "Alas! I have not found Him; I have not found Him; and I cannot be content until I do so!" Beloved, never sit down short of Christ; for short of Christ is short of salvation. Whatever you hear, never be content with hearing: long to find Him of whom you hear. However sweetly the story is told, the mere hearing of the truth must never be enough for you. You want for your salvation a personal Christ, to be heard by your own heart, and received by your own faith; and I entreat you never rest until this is your happy possession. Find HIM—Him whom your soul loves—Him in whom alone your soul may trust. Let not voices from heaven, if you could hear them, much less the voices of godly men and women on earth, ever content you, apart from the Lord Jesus Christ, who is all in all.

Furthermore, a soul *seeking Jesus is glad to confess Him.* It was awe-inspiring to behold angels arrayed in white; it was a rare boon for the Magdalene to gaze upon, those shining ones sitting in solemn state at the head and the foot of the spot where Jesus had once laid! But it did not so overpower Mary as to prevent her open acknowledgment of her Lord. When she spoke to Peter and John, in the second verse, she said, "They have taken away *the* Lord out of the sepulcher, but when she addressed the angels, she said, "They have taken away *my* Lord, and I know not where they have laid him." It might not be necessary to say, "*my* Lord" to the two apostles, who knew exactly what she was; but she had not seen those angels before, and she would not let them go without their knowing that Jesus was her Lord, her very own; and so she puts it, "They have taken away my Lord." I like that amazingly. Are you a seeking saint? Whether you see Him or do not see Him, He is still yours; and you must hold to it that He is still your own. "My beloved is mine, and I am his"; and if I do not just now behold the smilings of His face, yet He is my Lord. I have given myself up to Him; and, if He does not own me as His servant, I will still claim Him as my Master. Come what may, if I walk in darkness, I will cleave to Him the more closely, for I will not wander from Him. Whither should I go? If all heaven does not shine upon me, I shall still look up that way. I have fallen into a fog, and can scarcely see my way beyond my hand; but yet I am my Lord's for all that, and I am not ashamed to declare it. "Though he slay me, yet will I trust in him." His I am, and Him I serve. My ear has been bored to the doorpost, and I am His happy bondsman forever. Come death, come life, come darkness of soul, or joy of spirit; whatever happens, I am my Lord's. Such holy constancy will be rewarded.

In the true seeker, the one cry of the soul is Christ, none but Christ, Christ alone. Mary looks beyond all others. Angels may come, and angels may go; but she neither seeks nor fears them. She blushes not to confess her Lord before the white-robed spirits; but she seeks *Him*, and must find *Him*. O child of God, keep you to the one object of your search! O sinner, when once you feel your need of Jesus, bend all your desires toward Him, and seek Him alone! If all your search is after Jesus, you shall find Him. Let not a heaven of angels suffice to take you off from searching for your Lord and His salvation. O child of God, when you have lost the light of your Lord's face, feel that you must have it back again, or die in the dark; and when you thus feel, He will return to you. He never set a soul longing for Himself, and Himself only, without gratifying the longing which He had created. Hunger and thirst after the Lord Jesus are blessed; for He who created them will satisfy them. Oh, that the Lord would cause us to faint and pine after Himself more and more, and then visit us with that which is our soul's only fullness, namely, His precious, priceless Self!

A Soul Seeking Jesus May Have Him Very Near, and Not Know It

Read, "When she had thus said, she turned herself back, and saw Jesus standing, and knew not that it was Jesus." He was behind her while she stood looking into the sepulcher; and though she did not perceive it, *His presence operated upon her*. She had been speaking to the angels, and answering their question; and suddenly she was conscious that someone was standing just behind her. How came she thus to feel? Some think that, as Mark describes the angels as standing up, the Lord had, at that moment, come behind Mary, and the holy angels, perceiving their Lord, rose up to do Him honor. They had been sitting in contemplation at the place of His sepulcher, but as soon as they caught sight of their Lord, they stood up, as if to do His bidding. From their movements Mary concluded that someone was passing behind her. It may have been so; for assuredly the angelic guards would have paid Him instant reverence; but, on the other hand, rising is scarcely so much a method of saluting a superior in the East as it is in the West. Let us suggest something else. You have been sitting at your table, writing, and a friend has come behind you with noiseless tread, but yet on a sudden you have been aware of a presence. Before you had heard or seen you were impressed—what if I say overshadowed? Was it not so with Mary Magdalene and the Savior? I am not superstitious if I assert that something very similar happens to me when Jesus is near. Many a believer will tell you that he has, at times, when he has been in prayer, or hearing the Word, or meditating, felt as if he could be sure that the Lord stood near him. There could, of course, be no palpable impression upon the flesh; for now, after the flesh, know we Him no more; but yet His presence has impressed our souls. There are influences of mind on mind which are beyond the recognition of science. The great Spirit of our Lord has means of making itself spiritually known to our spirits—means which flesh and blood know nothing of, and which lips could not describe. I have discerned the special presence of my Lord with me by a consciousness as sure as that by which I know that I live. Jesus has been as real to me, at my side in this pulpit, as though I had beheld Him with my eyes. I appeal to the experience of many of you. Have you not been moved by a mysterious influence, which has overawed, inspired, and impressed you beyond description? A divine, majestic, delightful, and hallowing presence has been near you; and you have turned to look at a something which was so distinct that you would not have been surprised had it been visible to you. Mary did not discover at first that it was the Lord, but she felt His powerful influence, and then "she turned herself back, and saw Jesus."

The next thing to be noted was, that she saw Jesus standing. The word is better rendered "beholdeth," as in the Revised Version. It does not merely mean that she saw Him; but *His presence fixed her gaze*. She steadily observed Him. She could not take her eyes off; she beheld Him intently; for she seemed to say, "I must have seen that face before. Can it be He? It is wonderfully like; but the thought cannot be entertained." But she stood, and beheld Jesus with steadfast gaze. Thus would we hold our meditations fixed upon His person. This may be so; and yet we may not know that the Lord is with us, though we are conscious of more than human company. In the case of a seeking sinner, Jesus has really come to him, and has been comforting him, and yet he did not know that it was Jesus; but dreamed that He was far away. His soul felt so tender, so melted, so ready to yield, so near to God, that he was sure some holy power was ruling him; but he knew not that it was Jesus. Occasionally, you and I have known such secret touches of heart and conscience, with bright hope, and burning love, that we have wondered at ourselves, and yet we have not dared to believe that it was the Lord Himself who was thus at work upon us. And yet it was even so. We were looking for Jesus by His own light. Our hearts burned, and yet we did not perceive whence came the fire. Jesus may be very near, and yet we may fear that He has gone from us in anger.

What was it, do you think, that prevented her seeing and knowing her Lord? Shall we say that *her unbelief and sorrow dimmed her eyes*? Was it that, like the disciples on the road to Emmaus, her eyes were holden? Very possibly. Was it her tears that blinded her to the divine vision? Not so likely; for tears full often cleanse the spiritual vision. Weeping for an absent Christ has often made us quit a sin which aforetime had prevented fellowship with Jesus. What was it, then? I think it was that the sight was not what she expected. She was longing to see Jesus; but, maybe, she only hoped to see Him wrapped in grave clothes; and so, you notice, that the evangelist puts it, "She saw Jesus *standing,* and knew not that it was Jesus." If she had seen Him lying down, with the image of death upon His face, she would have known Him; but to see Jesus *standing,* was far more than she could have hoped for. She had seen His lifeless body taken down by Joseph and Nicodemus, and she had helped to wrap Him in spices and fine linen; but to see Him standing, alive, was more than she could have dreamed of. The rapture was too great for her to expect or believe; and we marvel not that it is written "she knew not that it was Jesus."

Beloved, our conceptions of our Lord are so poor and low, that if He were to come to us in even a moderated degree of His glory, we should fail to apprehend that it was really He. John knew Him, he had laid his head in His bosom, but he says, "When I saw him, I fell at his feet as dead." So overpoweringly beyond all that John could have expected, was the vision of the Lord in His glory. It is true the Lord Jesus did not manifest Himself in that manner to Mary; but still, the particular posture of standing was beyond what she looked for, and therefore He was not perceived. It may be, that the Lord Jesus is truly appearing to some sinner here; but as the appearance is not what he expected, he is unable to hope that it is his Savior. You are told simply to trust Him; and this is hardly what you looked for: you thought that you would suffer an experience of amazing sorrow. You looked for an affair which could be put into a biography. Tell me, did you not! But you will not have anything of the sort. You hear a voice which cries, "Only trust Him, only trust Him." Obey that voice, and enter into immediate rest. You thought that you would be driven to the verge of madness, and then be relieved with a joy which would make you dance; but instead thereof, you are led quietly to trust. So long as you are truly saved, what matters it? The Lord Jesus is present wherever there is humble faith in Him, for that plant never grows except where He sets His pierced foot. Believe, and then know that it is Jesus.

And you, dear brother, who have lost the presence of Christ a while, perhaps you expect Him to come tonight, and carry you away in a sacred transport; instead of which, it may be He will calm you, and fill you with repose, or He may even rebuke you, and send you out to work and suffer for Him. May you have the discernment, however your Lord may come, to know that it is the Lord! Though He comes not in the way in which you looked for Him, yet be not so purblind as to mistake Him for another. Yet if you should even think that your risen Lord is the gardener, you might not be so very wrong. If, under that misapprehension, you should ask Him to dress the garden of your heart, and pluck up your weeds, and water your plants, it would be well with you. Still, He may be near you, and yet you may not know Him. Take comfort from this fact; and though you mourn your own dullness of apprehension, do not utterly condemn yourself.

Under her misapprehension, Mary *did not catch the tone of our Lord's voice* when He asked her why she wept. Our Lord quoted the question of the angel, as if to show that He would gladly support the word which His servant had spoken. Happy messenger, whose words can be repeated by his Master! But yet Mary's ear was heavy, and she perceived not her Lord. Ah me! we also may be in such a state that we do not discern the blessed Lover of our souls, though He speaks in the language of consolation! We would have ventured to predict that never would Mary Magdalene have forgotten that dear voice; but she did so; and what wonder if *we* do the same?

In a word, she was so far from discovering her Lord that *she took Him to be her foe rather than her Friend.* She imagined that the gardener had borne the body away. Was he so unwilling to have a corpse within the region of his gardening that he had put it in a corner, that no one might perceive it? She humbles herself to him, and offers to carry away the form to which she feared he had such an objection. "Tell me where thou hast laid him, and I will take him away." He to whom she spoke had not taken away her treasure: He had brought it to her; yea, He was Himself that treasure! Beloved, you and I also have reckoned our best Friend to be our enemy; so foolish are we, and so soon mistaken. In the darkness of our souls we judge unrighteously, and complain of our Lord whom alone we ought to praise. He knows our ignorance, and He forgives.

A Soul Seeking Jesus Will Do Anything to Find Him

Mary Magdalene was still seeking; and when she saw one standing before her, whom she thought to be the gardener, what did she do? Why, she inquired of that gardener where she might find Him whom she loved. *She was willing to learn from anyone.* If you are in earnest to find the Lord Jesus, you will not be particular about where you go, or of whom you learn. No matter whether the preacher is a doctor of divinity or a converted coal-heaver, so long as he preaches Christ, you will be glad to learn from him. She supposed Him to be the gardener; but yet she said to Him, "Sir, if thou hast borne him hence, tell me where thou hast laid him." Many have been happy to learn of Jesus from fishermen and cobblers. Does my friend object to my hearing an illiterate man? Ah, sir! when I am seeking eternal salvation, I care little about the philosopher, I want the experimental Christian. For him I feel a deep respect; and, even if I know him to be only a gardener, I speak to him reverently as "Sir." When a man is not truly seeking the Lord, he wants short sermons, and these of a high literary order, or else adorned with attractive rhetoric; but when he is, with his whole heart, seeking for the Savior, he is not so concerned about polite phrases, and ecclesiastical correctness; but he looks eagerly for a practical direction how he may come to Jesus; and he will take that from any man or woman, be their station what it may. Let him be a chimney-sweep, if he will lead me to Jesus, I will follow. So it was with this holy woman; she desired to find the Lord, and she was altogether absorbed in that one pursuit. She speaks as if everybody was equally intent upon the one theme; for instead of mentioning the name Jesus, she says, "If thou hast borne him hence." Why, Mary, what are you talking about? "About Him," says she. But who is this of whom you speak? Ah, friends! to her there was but one "Him" in all the world, just then! Oh, to be thus absorbed!

Such was the desire of Magdalene to find the Lord Jesus, that *she feared no ghastly sight*. Let her know where the body is laid, and she will be there. That body, which had bled so much from its five wounds, must have been a heartbreaking sight to a tenderhearted woman; but she is not dismayed. Let the body be how it may, it is the flesh and blood of her dear Lord, and she must pay it homage. Wounds or no wounds, she would behold it. A wounded Christ is altogether lovely in the eyes of His redeemed. His blood, flowing for me, clothes Him with a royal crimson robe in my eyes. I fear nothing, so long as I may but come to Him. Dear hearts, if you long for salvation, you will not find fault with these who preach the doctrine of the cross, the wounds, the blood! You will not kick at the doctrine of a crucified Savior, your Substitute condemned at the bar of justice. You want Jesus who died. You must behold Him for yourself by faith, and no ridicule of the vain, or sneer of the proud, or cavil of the doubling, can make Him uncomely in your eyes.

Notice that *she dreads no heavy burden*. She says, "I will take him away." Why, Mary, you could not bear away so great a load! You would fall beneath the weight of a man's corpse! You are not strong enough for the sad task! Ah! but she thought that she could bear the blessed burden, and she meant to try! She would have accomplished it. Faith laughs at impossibility, and cries, "it shall be done"; but love actually performs the deed. A heart that is burning with love has about it a sevenfold energy, whose capacity it would be hard to calculate. It would seem a grim and terrible task for a woman, at early morning, to be carrying from its grave the corpse of one who had been hanged upon a tree; but she offers herself for the deed, and is even eager for it. To a soul that would fain find Christ, nothing is too hot or too heavy, nothing is too cold or too sickening. We would do anything, refuse nothing, and suffer everything, if we might but clasp Him in our arms, our Jesus and our all.

Yet was she wedded to her old mistake: she continued to seek the living among the dead, for *she looked again into the sepulcher*. Thus have I seen seeking souls cling to their original mistake, and follow up those erroneous but natural hopes which are surely doomed to disappointment. How do I know that Mary began to look again into that sepulcher? Observe that, in the sixteenth verse we read, "She turned herself, and saith unto him, Rabboni!" That is the second time she turned herself. The first time she turned, and looked at Jesus, whom she supposed to be the gardener. Now, if she had to turn again to see Him, she must, in the meanwhile, have faced in the old direction, and must, therefore, have been peering again into the empty tomb. That is the difficulty which we have with poor seekers when they are in their fits. We persuade them from looking to themselves and their feelings, but they are soon back again at that unprofitable work. We tell them, "He is not here, for He is risen. Look not to your own dead self, with its feelings and resolvings, for Jesus is not there." For a while they yield to us, and try to look to the Lord; but they do not know Him, and so their eyes insensibly return to the old place, looking again into the sepulcher of self, to find a living hope in the things of death. Still, even this mistaken persistency shows how anxious they are, and how desperately they are set upon finding salvation. Though they make serious mistakes, and even repeat them, yet they cannot give over; for nothing short of Christ will content them.

A Seeking Soul May Find Jesus Through One Word

We might be wise to clip our sermons down, and make them much shorter. Long discourses have often missed the mark; but our Lord's one word gave Mary all she sought. He said to her, "Mary"; and at once she knew Him, and cried, "Rabboni." Only one word! Jesus can preach a perfect sermon in one word. O dear friends, when you cannot say much to an anxious inquirer, say a single word. Who knows what that one word may do? When you cannot repeat a sermon, quote a verse. "A verse may hit Him whom a sermon flies." Do not think that strength lies in length: it is often the reverse.

Though Mary came to herself by one word, *that one word was from Jesus Himself.* He and the angels together had not comforted her with a sentence, but one word from His heart went to her heart. That one word of love from His lip, "Mary," brought that other word of reverence from her lip, "Rabboni." Dear friends, beseech the Lord to speak in His own all-powerful way at this time. In the meeting for prayer you prayed for me that I might speak, and I hope the Lord heard you; but now go yet further, and cry, "Speak, Lord! Speak Yourself! The angel of the church has spoken, and You have sealed his message, but now, we entreat You, go further, and do speak one word Yourself, by thine own Spirit!"

That one word was the Magdalene's own name. It was as though He had said, "I have called you by your name: you are Mine." Words, when they are spoken with a general bearing, may prove feeble. When the angel said, "Woman," and Jesus Himself said, "Woman," that name belonged to a large class of individuals; and Mary did not take it to herself. But when our Lord said, "Mary," there was but one Mary present, and therefore it came home to her without fail. This is what is needed: an assured, personal application of the Word. This our Lord grants when the message comes right home to you, as if you were the only one present: the preacher looks at you, speaks to you, and gives such personal details, that you are sure that not the preacher, but the preacher's God, is speaking to you. Then it is that you find the Lord, and know of a surety that it is He.

That word from the Master's lips, that word your own name, *that word shall wake the echoes of your heart* by arousing happy memories, and recalling hours of sweet delight. When a soul knows that Jesus knows its name, it soon begins to know Jesus for itself. Who but He could have said, "Mary" with that emphatic accent, with that peculiar intonation? Who but He could have brought all her life to remembrance, not so much by the word itself as by the meaning which He threw into it, and the vivid flash of His eye which went with it? One glance of His eye darted the light of God into her spirit. "Mary!" was the Open Sesame of her heart and mind. Oh, now she has Him! Lord, speak in this fashion to some seeker who is here looking for You! Lord, speak to John and Peter, to Jane and Sarah! Let the message come to many hearers from Your own lips, to Your own glory!

A Seeking Soul Will Respond with Reverence to the Word of Jesus

Mary said at once, "Rabboni." This is a Hebrew word, signifying "Master," or, as Parkhurst says, having a Chaldee particle within it, which makes it to mean "My Master," or, as I have heard some say, "*Great* Master." At any rate, she meant that *He was her Lord and Teacher*. He knew her heart, He understood her inmost soul, and therefore she owned Him Lord. He had called her by her name, and she owned that all-controlling voice. He was her Master, since He could so divinely know and move her heart. Even thus may we each one say, "My God, my Savior, convinced by Your knowledge of me, and overpowered by Your condescension toward me, I feel that You have the sole right to my love, my trust, my obedience! You are within and about me, nearer to me than hands and feet, nearer to me than even the blood that flows from my heart; and therefore I joyfully submit my whole being to You, to be ruled and instructed by You as my sole Lord and Rabbi!"

In addition to this, *she feels that she knows Him*. He is no stranger to her. Had He been a stranger, He might have said "Mary" many times; but because He was the Good Shepherd that knows His sheep, and calls them by name, therefore Mary, as one of His sheep, responded to His call. Mary knew Him: do you know the Master? Beloved, do you know the Lord Jesus? To know Him is life eternal! Have you this life? Not to know Him is an ignorance dark as death. I do not say, do you know *about* Him? But do you know HIM? Has the Lord ever spoken to you? Has He ever worded it with you? Has He spoken one almighty syllable which has thrilled your very soul? If so, you will at once take Him to be your Teacher, and yield your intellect to His instruction. Henceforth you will only want to know what He chooses to reveal; but what He reveals will satisfy your reason at once. Henceforth opposing philosophies will go to the wind, and you will learn of Him. Henceforth your own thoughts and speculations will seem as the chaff of the threshing floor, compared with the words which He teaches, which are full of weight and divine authority, even of light and power eternal. Tonight, from my very heart, I call Jesus "Rabboni." I will have no Rabbi but Christ; no Master but my Lord Jesus. By all His knowledge of me, and all His revelation of Himself to me, I take Him to be to me my Teacher and Lord.

"Rabboni" means also *"Master" by way of authority.* Mary confessed herself the follower of Jesus. Where He led the way, she was resolved to follow, even as our hymn puts it—

> I am thine, and thine alone,
> This I gladly, fully own;
> And, in all my works and ways,
> Only now would seek thy praise.

From that time, even if it had not been so with her before, Mary Magdalene was one of those of whom it could be said, "They follow the Lamb whithersoever he goeth." Happy man and happy woman, who will keep close to every footstep of the Lord. If you are seeking Him at this hour, pray that, at this moment, He may speak the revealing word, so that you may henceforth feel that a change has come over you, the like of which you have never known. May you experience a sacred twist which shall affect your whole character! May Jesus touch your heart so that your whole body, soul, and spirit shall never forget that touch in time or in eternity! Amen.

Additional Volumes in the

C. H. Spurgeon Sermon Series

Spurgeon's Sermons on the Cross of Christ

These sermons provide a varied look at the death of Christ on the cross, its meaning, its significance, and its power in the life of the believer. The depth of insight is Spurgeon at his best— expounding the Word of God with insight and passion.

ISBN 0-8254-3687-7 160 pp. paperback

Spurgeon's Sermons on New Testament Men • Book One

In this sermon collection Kregel Publications has assembled a biblical portrait gallery of New Testament men, including sermons on John the Baptist, the man with the withered hand, Pilate, Stephen, and Simeon. As always, pastors and speakers will find ample "food for thought" in Spurgeon's exposition as well as "seed thoughts" to help in sermon preparation. Christian readers will find encouragement in Spurgeon's insight into the practical issues of Christian living.

ISBN 0-8254-3783 160 pp. paperback

Spurgeon's Sermons on Old Testament Men • Book One

One of Spurgeon's favorite presentations was the biographical sermon, drawing upon both the faithfulness and the failures of biblical characters. Includes sermons on Abraham, Moses, David, and Daniel.

ISBN 0-8254-3772-5 160 pp. paperback

Spurgeon's Sermons on Old Testament Women • Book One

In this sermon collection Kregel Publications has assembled a biblical portrait gallery of Old Testament women including sermons on Eve, Sarah, Ruth, and Esther

ISBN 0-8254-3781-4 160 pp. paperback

Spurgeon's Sermons on the Resurrection

A insightful set of sermons on the power and significance of the resurrection of Jesus Christ. These messages will challenge and encourage the believer to live the resurrection life of Christ.

ISBN 0-8254-3686-9 160 pp. paperback

Spurgeon's Sermons on Soulwinning

A new collection of Spurgeon's sermons on the means and methods of bringing the lost to Christ.

ISBN 0-8254-3787-3 160 pp. 8.99p

Spurgeon's Sermons on Special Days and Occasions

A special collection of Spurgeon's sermons for Christmas, Easter, and other special days of the Christian year.

ISBN 0-8254-3786-5 160 pp. 8.99p